Healthy Taste

of life

WHOLESOME GLUTEN FREE DAIRY FREE RECIPES

OLGA DEEZ

Contents

Desserts

Beverages (Hot & Cold)

Dressings And Sauces

Breads Rolls Tortillas

Miscellaneous

Introduction

Disappointed by most gluten free and dairy free products on the market, I decided to create my own. All baked goods (breads, cakes, cookies) are all made without preservatives, dough conditioners, gums, or flavor enhancers. Also in order to keep the ingredients as clean as possible I used gluten free sourdough starter in recipes that require leavening.

Though all of the recipes in this book are dairy free, gluten free, corn free and soy free. Some of them are paleo or whole30 friendly. Plus a few vegan options for those who want to limit meat and eggs. Each recipe in this book is loaded with essential vitamins, minerals, healthier fats, without refined sugar and no highly processed foods or additives. In addition, it also includes the nutritional profile of every recipe and several key tips on choosing high quality gluten free and dairy free ingredients (with links). Everything was tested and tried personally, no sponsored content here.

Even though eating whole foods and cutting out all sugars, grains, legumes and dairy (specific for paleo and whole30 diets) is very helpful for detecting subtle food intolerances, reducing inflammation or healing the digestive tract, it's restrictiveness might be hard to follow in the long run. Some people may cave in and start back with unhealthy foods or become obsessed with their way of eating.

Therefore I included a variety of recipes, some suitable for whole30 or paleo and some that include gluten free grains, legumes and dairy free alternatives. So whenever you feel like quitting or having a sweet craving some time to time, or need a celebration dessert made with clean ingredients – the book will help you maintain a healthy balanced diet.

I've tried all elimination diets available and they all have positive effect in the short run. But I found that the key to maintaining your way of eating under control is access to (healthier) alternatives whenever you need them. There is no harm in having a slice of homemade (wholegrain) bread with your soup. The satisfaction is important too for maintaining a healthy relationship with your food.

By switching over to whole foods and healthy carbohydrates and fat (even though they are gluten and dairy free), it can be liberating. There is no need to count calories, fat grams or carbs. This way of eating provides all the nutrition you need, and overall helps you think less about food, body image and staying mentally healthy.

All recipes are categorized according to the type of diet they are compliant with:

GF - Gluten free; DF - Dairy free; V - Vegan; P - Paleo; W30 - Whole30

This book is more inclined for those who have tried gluten and dairy free cooking before, but who want less refined ingredients. It is intended for those who want a more nutritious, wholesome approach, not just food looking highly processed foods with empty calories. Those who are used to heavily processed food in the grocery stores, might find these recipes unsatisfactory, because they don't have additives, excessive sugar and artificial taste enhancing agents.

The main reason I'm concentrating on real food ingredients is because most gluten-free (and some dairy free) foods are often not organic and made with flours and/or starches and processed sugars that contain GMOs - which don't bring any nutritional benefit. These include tapioca starch, potato starch, corn starch, soy lecithin, canola or soybean oil. And when used alone, these ingredients make seemingly healthy foods unhealthy

My Gluten Free + Dairy Free Essential Food Staples

Organic Gluten Free Flours:

Gluten free rolled oats (ground into flour)
Sprouted brown rice flour; Sweet brown rice flour; White rice flour
Sorghum flour; Teff flour
Buckwheat flour
Arrowroot flour; Cassava flour
Tigernut flour; Almond flour

Organic Non-dairy Alternatives:

Vegan cultured butter (Miyoko's)
Harmless Harvest yogurts
Forager Project: cashew yogurt
Forager Project: coconut cashew oat milk
Homemade tigernut coconut milk
Trader Joe's canned coconut milk
Trader Joe's canned coconut cream
Coconut Whipping Cream
Condensed Coconut Milk
Enjoy Life Dairy free chocolate chips
Enjoy Life Dairy free chocolate chunks

Organic Oils:

Avocado oil; Extra virgin olive oil
Cold pressed hemp seed oil
Coconut oil

Organic Raw Nuts And Seeds:

Almonds, Walnuts, Pecans, Cashews
Brown flax seeds & golden flax seeds
Chia seeds
Pumpkin seeds; Sunflower seeds
Hemp seeds; Sesame seeds
Caraway seeds; Coriander seeds

Sweeteners And Other

Maple syrup; Maple sugar; Maple butter
Coconut sugar; Stevia extract powder
Vanilla extract; Ground Vanilla Bean Powder

Dried and Freeze Dried Fruits

Medjool dates, Cranberries, Prunes, Raisins
Freeze dried fruit

Other:

Apple sauce, Tomato paste
Psyllium husk

Seasonings:

Himalayan pink salt; Celtic sea salt
Organic brown mustard, Dijon mustard
Cococnut liquid aminos

The products mentioned above are easily found on Amazon and most of health food store across the U.S.

Breakfasts

· ·

Clean gluten free dairy free breakfast ideas loaded with nutrients to keep your energy steady until noon. Choose from egg dishes, oatmeal, granola, pancakes, muffins, crepes and savory recipes that are practical to eat and easy to make ahead.

Grain Free Nut Free Granola

Crunchy gluten free granola that is also low carb, paleo, vegan, dairy free & oil free. Enjoy it on its own or serve it with dairy free milk, yogurt, smoothie or ice cream.

Course: Breakfast   Makes 6 cups   Ready in 1h 30 minutes   GF, DF, V, P, W30

INGREDIENTS

6 oz sliced tigernuts
1/2 cup sunflower seeds, raw
1/2 cup pumpkin seeds, raw
1/2 cup flax seeds, ground
1/3 cup hemp seeds
1/4 cup chia seeds
1/2 cup coconut chips, raw
1/2 cup coconut cream
1/3 cup maple syrup or maple sugar (omit if whole30)
1 cup dried unsweetened cranberries - (soaked) or any other dried berries
1 tsp vanilla extract
1/4 tsp pink Himalayan salt

Add-ons (optional)

1/3 cup freeze dried raspberries - crushed
1/3 cup freeze dried bananas - crushed

DIRECTIONS

1. Prepare the ingredients that need soaking. Take tigernuts, sunflower seeds, pumpkin seeds and hemp seeds and soak them in a bowl of water for at least 1 hour. In a separate bowl soak the dried fruit in warm water as well. This will help remove dirt and any oil or sugar residue.

2. Assemble the granola. Preheat oven to 280 F (137C). Line a baking tray with parchment paper. Into a large bowl toss all ingredients (drained) and dry ingredients except the coconut chips. Add the coconut cream (room temperature) or oil, the sweetener (if you use any) and vanilla extract. Use a spatula to stir and combine.

Spread the granola mixture evenly on the prepared baking tray (in a single thin layer or use two baking trays if needed).

3. Bake the granola. Bake for 1 hour or so, stirring halfway through. Add the coconut chips for the last 10-15 minutes of baking (they get burnt easily). Your granola is ready when is slightly golden brown. To make it crispier, turn off the oven and let it sit inside with the door a few inches open (about 30 min).

4. Final mix-ins. When it's completely cooled, stir in the dried freeze fruits (I used raspberries and bananas).

Transfer your cool granola into a glass jar. Store up to 3-4 weeks. This recipe makes about 5-6 cups of granola.

Serving size: 1 cup without freeze dried fruit: Calories: 534.8 g; Total Fat: 30.1 g; Total carbohydrate: 59.6 g; Fiber: 19.5 g; Protein: 15.1 g; Sugar: 35 g; Vitamin A: 0 %; Vitamin C: 0 %; Iron: 19.1 %; Calcium: 4.3 %; Magnesium 27.4 %; Zinc: 16.8 %.

Berry Smoothie Oat Bowl

The base in this breakfast bowl is a berry smoothie, served with a few spoons of cooked oatmeal, topped with nuts and seeds for crunchiness. No added sugar here, just real fruit.

Course: Breakfast   Makes 2 servings   Ready in 15 minutes   GF, DF, V

INGREDIENTS

Oatmeal

1 cup rolled oats (gluten free)
2 cups water (or plant milk)
salt to taste

Smoothie

1 medium banana
1/2 cup strawberries (halves)
1/2 cup blueberries
1/2 cup blackberries
1/2 cup plant based yogurt
(plain unsweetened version)

Toppings

1 tsp chia seeds
1 tsp hemp seeds
1 tbsp pumpkin seeds
10 almonds (sliced)
1 tsp ground flax seeds
1 tbsp coconut chips

DIRECTIONS

1. Cook the oatmeal. Combine oats, water and salt in a medium saucepan. Bring to a boil, then reduce heat to low. Simmer uncovered for 3 to 5 minutes until thickened, stirring occasionally. Remove from heat and let cool slightly.

2. Make the smoothie. In a blender mix together the fruits and yogurt scraping down sides if needed, until smooth. You can either use fresh fruits or frozen, it's up to you.

3. Assemble the bowl. Pour the smoothie into two bowls. Add a few tablespoons of cooked oatmeal in each bowl and top with seeds and nuts.

Notes And Suggestions

To save time, make the oat porridge the day before and store in the fridge. In the morning just make the smoothie and assemble the bowl

Serving size: 1 bowl: Calories: 600 g; Total Fat: 28.1 g; Total carbohydrate: 70.6 g; Fiber: 14.3; Protein: 15.1 g; Sugars: 19.3 g; Vitamin A: 2.4%; Vitamin B-6: 22.6%; Vitamin C: 48.4%; Iron: 27.2%; Calcium: 7.3 %; Magnesium: 20.6%.

Cranberry Banana Muffins

Soft and fluffy cranberry banana muffins made with sweet ripe bananas, dried cranberries and whole grain gluten free flours. This can also be baked as a loaf.

Course: Breakfast   Makes 9 muffins   Ready in 40 minutes   GF, DF

INGREDIENTS

1/4 cup plant milk
2 large ripe bananas
2 large eggs
2 tbsp of avocado oil or coconut oil
1 tsp vanilla extract
3 tbsp maple sugar, or other sugar, or use stevia
1 ⅓ cup gluten free whole grain flour blend 1
(see page 274)
1 tsp baking soda
1 ½ tsp apple cider vinegar
1/6 tsp pink salt
1 tsp cinnamon
1 cup dried cranberries
2 tbsp chia seeds

DIRECTIONS

1. Preheat oven to 400 F. In a large bowl, mash the bananas with a fork then whisk together the other wet ingredients (milk, eggs, oil, vanilla) until combined. Then add the dry ingredients, mixing until they are fully incorporated. Then fold in the cranberries and chia seeds, mixing just until combined.

2. Just before baking, add the baking soda + apple cider vinegar and give it one final gentle mix. If you add this too early the bubbles might disperse by the time you need to bake.

3. Divide the batter evenly among paper lined muffin tins, filling each tin all the way to the top.

4. Lower the temperature to 375 F and bake for 30 minutes, or until the tops are puffed up and golden brown.

5. Cool muffins 5 minutes in the pan before transferring to a cooling rack. Enjoy the muffins warm, or store in a covered container for up to 2 days. Freeze for up to 3 months.

Notes And Suggestions

Replace the oil with any vegan butter if you have to.

Use the suggested gluten free flour mix for a healthier treat, or use your favorite gluten free flour blend. If the dough will seem too wet add some more flour.

Serving size: 1 muffin: Calories: 203.3 g; Total Fat: 6.3 g; Total carbohydrate: 31.9 g; Protein: 4.9 g; Sugars: 14 g; Vitamin A: 3.1 % Vitamin C: 11.8 %; Iron: 8.2 %; Calcium: 5.5 %; Vitamin B-6: 11.4%.

Bacon And Egg Breakfast Hash

This hearty delicious breakfast consists of perfectly fried bacon and egg, slices of avocado, fresh greens and crispy browned hash brown finished with a drizzle of creamy basil sauce. Perfect for those looking for a more caloric breakfast.

Course: Breakfast   Makes 1 serving   Ready in 20 minutes   GF, DF, P, W30

INGREDIENTS

2 medium potatoes, grated
1/4 medium onion, grated (or use onion powder)
1/6 tsp pink salt
pinch of black pepper
1 large egg, fried with a pinch of salt
2 slices of organic bacon (turkey or pork)
1/2 medium avocado, sliced
handful of greens like spinach
2-3 tbsp creamy basil pesto sauce (see page 234)

DIRECTIONS

1. Toss the grated potatoes in a bowl and cover with cold water until you shred the onion. This step removes excess starch and helps the potato to crisp. Then transfer both in a mesh bag or cloth and squeeze out the liquid as much as possible.

2. In a 9 inch skillet over medium high heat cook the bacon and the egg, remove from skillet and place on a plate. In the same skillet (with bacon fat) spread out the fully dried grated potatoes and onion so they cover the skillet bottom entirely. The layer should not be too thick, about ¼ inch. Season with salt and pepper and press down the potatoes with a spatula to flatten out the top and the edges. Reduce heat to medium and continue cooking until golden brown and crisp 7 to 8 minutes.

3. To flip the hash brown without breaking you need to cover the skillet with a large plate and quickly flip side up, onto the plate. Then slide hash brown back into pan. Continue to cook over medium heat until the other side is golden brown and crisp, 5 to 6 minutes longer.

4. When ready slide the hash brown in the same plate, top with egg, bacon, sliced avocado, some greens and finish with a drizzle of basil sauce. Fold the potato round in half, and serve while warm.

Notes And Suggestions

Use sweet potatoes if you like, and your favorite sauce.

Serving size: all: Calories: 971.1 g; Total Fat: 52.8 g; Total carbohydrate: 96.4; Fiber: 22.1 g; Protein: 38.2 g; Sugars: 5.7 g; Vitamin A: 29.4 %; Vitamin B-6: 92.9 %; Vitamin C: 89.2 %; Iron: 44.4 %; Calcium: 14.2 %; Magnesium: 57.1 %; Zinc: 29.2 %.

Vegan Gluten Free Sourdough Pancakes

Create fluffy pancakes without using eggs or milk. The gluten free sourdough starter and the right flour mix helps to acquire a delicious flavor, the right texture and a nice golden brown color. This recipe is perfect for using your sourdough starter discard.

Course: Breakfast   Makes 10 (3.5") pancakes   Ready in 25 minutes   GF, DF, V

INGREDIENTS

1 cup sourdough starter
(for recipe see page 280)
1/2 cup plant yogurt (I used Harmless Harvest)
1/4 cup flour blend no. 2 (see page 276)
1/2 tsp psyllium husk + 3 tbsp water (to form a gel)
2 tbsp melted vegan butter
2 tbsp maple sugar
1 tsp vanilla extract
1 tsp apple cider vinegar or lemon juice
3/4 tsp baking soda
pinch of salt

DIRECTIONS

1. In a large bowl, whisk together sourdough starter, plant yogurt, melted butter, vanilla extract, apple cider vinegar and the psyllium husk + water mixture (it sits a bit and gels up - use as egg replacer). Add the flour mix, sugar and salt, mix until smooth.

2. Just before cooking add the baking soda and give it one final gentle mix. If you add this too early the bubbles might disperse by the time you need to cook the pancakes.

3. If you're using a non stick ceramic skillet, then no oil is needed for cooking. Scoop 2-3 tbsp of pancake mixture onto skillet and spread into a circle. Cook until you see bubbles forming around the edge and flip. Cook another minute or so.

Serve with maple syrup, fruits or anything else you like.

Notes And Suggestions

Use the suggested gluten free flour mix for a healthier breakfast, or use your favorite gluten free flour blend. For fluffier pancakes some use baking powder, but I prefer to avoid it.

Taste the first batch of pancakes and adjust the sweetness to your liking. Use coconut oil or cream if you can't find a good vegan butter.

Serving size: 1 pancake: Calories: 117.2 g; Total Fat: 5.7 g; Total carbohydrate: 16.4 g; Protein: 1.9 g; Sugars: 1.3 g; Vitamin A: %; Vitamin C: 0 %; Iron: 2.3 %; Calcium: 1.2 %; Vitamin E: 0.6%; Magnesium: 6.3; Zinc: 3%.

Blueberry Muffins With Crumble Topping

Soft, fluffy, not overly sweet muffins, full of juicy blueberry deliciousness. Fort extra flavor these muffins are finished with a sweet and crunchy cinnamon streusel. You can also make a loaf.

Course: Breakfast   Makes 9-10 muffins   Ready in 45 minutes   GF, DF

INGREDIENTS

First mix these ingredients

(let them soak for 5 minutes)
1/2 cup plant milk
1 large egg – or make a flax "egg" if you want them vegan
1 cup apple sauce
6 tbsp plant based butter, or oil
1 ½ tsp apple cider vinegar
1 tsp vanilla extract
1 cup rolled oats (gluten free)

Then add the rest

3/4 cup sorghum flour
1/2 cup maple sugar, or coconut sugar
1 tsp baking soda
1/3 tsp pink salt
1 cup blueberries

Streusel topping

1/4 cup maple sugar
1 tbsp sorghum flour, or any other gluten free flour
1 tbsp avocado oil
1/3 tsp cinnamon
2 tbsp of oats, or nuts. I used sliced tigernuts

DIRECTIONS

1. Preheat the oven to 400 degrees F. If necessary, lightly grease the muffin cups or add cupcake liners. Set aside.

2. In a mixing bowl, combine the ingredients mentioned in the first column, mix well. Let them soak for 5-7 min. Add the rest of ingredients except baking soda. It should be mixed last.

3. Spoon the batter into the prepared muffin tins, filling each about three-fourths full.

4. Prepare the crumble topping. Add all ingredients in a small bowl. Mix with a fork to combine. Sprinkle the topping evenly on top of the unbaked muffins.

5. Bake the muffins at 400 F for 10 minutes then reduce the temperature to 375 F and bake for another 25 minutes until golden brown. (This will prevent the crumble topping from browning too much).

Notes And Suggestions

Toss the blueberries in the dry flour before mixing all with wet ingredients. This will keep the blueberries from sinking to the bottom.

Over mixing the batter can cause tough muffins. This is because you ruin the air bubbles.

Fresh blueberries or frozen, both work. Be warned that if you choose frozen, the muffin batter may turn purple.

Serving size: 1 muffin: Calories: 191.3; Total Fat: 8.8 g; Total carbohydrate: 22.6 g; Sugars: 14.9 g; Fiber: 2.4 g; Vitamin A: 45 % Vitamin C: 4.3 %; Iron: 1%; Calcium: 6 %.

Savory Sweet Potato Waffles

Light Belgian style waffles made with grated sweet potatoes, eggs, grain free flours and seasonings. These are great for quick breakfasts or brunches, as a cold snack or used as the 'bread' for a sandwich.

Course: Breakfast   Makes 2 (8") waffles   Ready in 30 minutes   GF, DF, P, W30

INGREDIENTS

2 cups grated sweet potatoes (packed)
3 large eggs
1/4 cup melted vegan butter or oil
1/2 cup almond flour (or tigernut flour)
2 tbsp ground flax seeds
2 tbsp arrowroot powder
1 tsp smoked paprika
1 tsp onion powder
1 tsp garlic powder
1/4 tsp Celtic sea salt
1 tsp mustard powder
3/4 tsp baking soda
1 tsp apple cider vinegar (or lemon juice)

Serve with:

fried egg, green onions, leafy greens, cherry tomatoes and a drizzle of homemade ranch dressing (see page 226)

DIRECTIONS

1. Set waffle iron to preheat. In a bowl combine grated potatoes with eggs, melted vegan butter (or oil) and mix to combine.

2. Then to that add all the other (dry) ingredients. Baking soda and apple cider vinegar should be added just before you're ready to make the waffles, it produces bubbles that don't stay active for too long.

3. Spread batter onto the waffle iron (I used a Belgian style iron) to fill in all of the crevices. Depending on the size and style of your waffle iron, you may make fewer or more waffles.

4. Let cook for 5-6 minutes at low temperature. Check waffle and continue to cook if needed. Waffles should be golden brown and slightly crisp.

Notes And Suggestions

You can add to your batter: bacon, herbs, seeds and basically anything you like.

Grease your waffle iron if it's necessary, non-stick irons don't require that.

Even though on whole30 diet you can have almond flour and arrowroot powder, they are not considered appropriate in baking, so it's up to you how badly you want these waffles.

Serving size: 1 (8 inch) waffle round: Calories: 635.8 g; Total Fat: 38 g; Total carbohydrate: 45 g; Protein: 19.6 g; Sugars: 6.9 g Vitamin A: 541.7 %; Vitamin C: 51.1 %; Iron: 20 %; Calcium: 13.5 %; Vitamin B-6: 27.5%; Vitamin E: 36.9 %.

Yogurt & Granola Parfait

These delicious breakfast parfaits will start your day off on the right foot. They are filled with plant yogurt, layered with fruit and grain free granola. Pretty, healthy and fun to eat, mix and match ingredients to make the perfect combination for you. Make ahead for busy mornings.

Course: Breakfast   Serves 2   Ready in 5 minutes   GF, DF, V, P, W30

INGREDIENTS

1 cup granola (see page 8)
1 cup plant based yogurt (plain version)
6 strawberries, sliced
16 raspberries
16 blueberries
8 blackberries

DIRECTIONS

1. Spoon 2-3 tbps of grain free granola into two 12 oz mason jars or glasses. Add 2-3 tbsp plant yogurt (use plain, unsweetened for less sugar). Top with fruits.

2. Repeat with another layer of granola, yogurt and fruits.

Notes And Suggestions

Fruit such as blueberries, strawberries, or raspberries are perfect for a breakfast parfait. But you could add bananas, pineapple, peaches, mango or anything you like.

Customize it with your favorite nuts or nut butters if you prefer a more filling version.

Store the parfaits in the fridge (covered) for up to 2-3 days.

Serving size: 12 oz jar: Calories: 654.1 g; Total Fat: 48.6 g; Total carbohydrate: 49.6 g; Protein: 14.2 g; Sugars: 21.3 g; Vitamin A 1.6 %; Vitamin C: 49.2 %; Iron: 17.2 %; Calcium: 6.7 %; Vitamin B-6: 4.4 %; Magnesium: 24.1 %; Zinc: 10.9%; Vitamin E: 2.3 %.

Green Veggie Omelette

A veggie packed breakfast that delivers protein and lots of nutrients. This omelette is kale blitzed with eggs in a food processor, sprinkled with fresh tomatoes, asparagus and leeks.

Course: Breakfast   Serves 1   Ready in 15 minutes   GF, DF, P, W30

INGREDIENTS

3 large eggs
3-4 large kale leaves
1/3 cup leeks, chopped
3-4 cherry tomatoes, chopped
3-4 asparagus spears, chopped
red onion wedge, sliced
pinch of black pepper
pinch of salt
1 tbsp olive oil, extra virgin

DIRECTIONS

1. Preheat a non stick frying pan (9"), on medium heat. Whilst pan is heating, in a food blender, add 3 eggs, kale and leeks and mix until it looks like bright green liquid.

2. Prepare the veggies. Chop or dice the asparagus, tomatoes and some red onion (optional).

3. Add some oil to the hot pan and gently pour in the blender content. Sprinkle the chopped veggies all over the omelette, also add salt and pepper for seasoning. Let heat it through for 5-7 minutes, on a low-medium heat. Cover with a lid after 1 minute to create some steam on top.

4. Using a large silicon spatula, carefully remove from pan and place onto a plate. It's ok if it breaks (the omelette is fragile), pile the pieces on plate and serve while warm.

Notes And Suggestions

You can also add some meat, other herbs and leafy greens, seeds and basically anything you like.

Serving size: whole omelette: Calories: 410.3 g; Total Fat: 27.7 g; Total carbohydrate: 20.8 g; Protein: 23.2 g; Sugars: 3.5 g; Fiber 4.4 g; Vitamin A: 332.9 %; Vitamin C: 220.6 %; Iron: 20 %; Calcium: 23.9 %; Vitamin B-6: 7.1 %; Vitamin E: 36.9 %.

Egg Free Omelette

A budget friendly, egg free omelette inspired by Indian cuisine. It tastes and looks almost like a real omelette and is packed with veggies and protein - to keep you full and satisfied longer.

Course: Breakfast   Serves 2   Ready in 25 minutes   GF, DF, V

INGREDIENTS

Makes 2 large omelettes:

1 cup moong dal (split Mung beans), soaked
1 cup non dairy milk or water
1/2 medium onion, chopped
3 tbsp fresh parsley, chopped
1/8 tsp black pepper
1/2 smoked paprika
1/8 tsp turmeric for color
1/2 tsp Celtic sea salt

Omelette filling (divide for two omelettes):

1/2 red onion, sliced
1 bell pepper, chopped
3 heads baby bok choy
10 cherry tomatoes
2 tbsp avocado oil
2 garlic clove, minced
1 tsp coconut aminos
salt and pepper to taste
vegan cheese, optional

DIRECTIONS

1. Soak 1/2 cup dried mung beans with 3-4 cups of water overnight or at least 6 hours in advance. Rinse well and discard the liquid.

2. Prepare the "omelette" base. In a blender mix the soaked beans (soaking will expand the beans, you should have aprox. 1 cup) and the milk (or water). Blend for a minute, then let it rest for 10 minutes and blend again for another minute. The mixture should be smooth and fluffy, like a crepe batter.

3. Transfer the bean mixture into a bowl, add the chopped onion, parsley, and the seasonings. Mix to incorporate.

4. Wash and chop the veggies for the filling. Preheat a non-stick frying pan (9"), on medium-high heat. Drizzle with oil and add the onion, garlic and bell pepper, sauté for 2-3 minutes, then add the bok choy (individual leaves) tomatoes and coconut aminos. Remove half of the veggies and save for another omelette.

5. Gently pour over the mung bean mixture. Let heat it through for 2 minutes, (this is the time to sprinkle some vegan cheese if you like, then cover with a lid and reduce to low heat, cook for 10 minutes.

6. Using a large silicon spatula, remove from pan and place onto a plate. Or if you like it very crispy flip on the other side and cook uncovered for another 5-7 minutes.

Notes And Suggestions

Moong Dal are split and skinned mung beans. You can find them in Indian stores, Whole Foods and online. You can also use the green mung beans (with skin) if you don't mind the color.

You can refrigerate the batter as well as the cooked omelette for up to 2 days. The batter might separate slightly, just blend before use.

Serving size: 1 omelette: Calories: 296.9 g; Total Fat: 17 g; Total carbohydrate: 29.7 g; Protein: 8.5 g; Sugars: 8.4 g; Fiber: 4.7 g; Vitamin A: 96 %; Vitamin B-6: 23.2; Vitamin C: 195.7 %; Iron: 6.3 %; Calcium: 3.6 %; Magnesium: 12.5 %.

Butternut Squash Pancakes

Fluffy pancakes made with mashed butternut squash blended with grain free gluten free flours, eggs, dairy free milk and finished with a sweet and sour taste due to cranberries.

Course: Breakfast   Makes 8 pancakes   Ready in 30 minutes   GF, DF, P, W30

INGREDIENTS

3/4 cup butternut squash puree
2 large eggs
4 tbsp non-dairy milk
1 tbsp avocado oil
3 tbsp cassava flour
3 tbsp tigernut flour (or almond flour)
1/4 cup dried cranberries
1/2 tsp cinnamon
1/2 tsp baking soda
1/2 tsp apple cider vinegar or lemon juice
pinch of salt
pinch of stevia extract (for sweetness)

Topping:

1/2 cup butternut squash, cubed
2 tbsp dried cranberries
1/4 tsp cinnamon
1 tbsp maple syrup (omit if whole30)
pinch of salt

DIRECTIONS

1. To make the butternut squash puree, peel the skin, cut into cubes and roast in the oven at 380F, covered, until fork tender. Then mash it with a fork or a food processor. Or use canned butternut squash puree.

2. In a bowl combine the wet ingredients: butternut squash puree, the eggs, the non dairy milk, the avocado oil, mix well.

3. Then add the dry ingredients: flours, cinnamon, salt, baking soda, stevia extract and mix well. Use a hand mixer for fluffier pancakes. Fold in the cranberries.

4. At the end add the apple cider vinegar and give it another gentle mix to activate the baking soda.

5. If you're using a non stick skillet, then no oil is needed. Using a 1/ cup measuring cup, scoop pancake mixture onto skillet and spread into a circle. Cook the bottom until it is golden brown and flip.

6. Serve with maple syrup, roasted butternut squash cubes, and cranberries. Enjoy!

Notes And Suggestions

To make the topping, roast some butternut squash cubes uncovered, sprinkle with cinnamon and a pinch of salt, add cranberries at the end. If you prefer some extra sweetness, sprinkle with coconut sugar or drizzle with maple syrup.

Serving size: 4 large pancakes: Calories: 362.5; Total Fat: 18.1 g; Total carbohydrate: 43.6 g; Protein: 10.0 g; Sugars: 18.5 g; Vitamin A: 8.5 %; Vitamin C: 8.3 %; Iron: 5.8 %; Calcium: 6.7 %.

Cinnamon Swirl Pancakes

Light and fluffy pancakes that taste like cinnamon rolls - loaded with cinnamon flavor, and topped with a delicious dairy free glaze. Enjoy them for a special breakfast or dessert!

Course: Breakfast   **Makes 10 pancakes**   **Ready in 1 hour**   GF, DF

INGREDIENTS

Pancake batter:

2 cups lightweight flour blend (see page 272)
1/2 cup apple sauce
1/2 cup plant milk
2 eggs
2 tsp vanilla extract
2 tbsp maple sugar
1 tsp baking soda
1 tsp apple cider vinegar
pinch of salt

Cinnamon swirl:

1/4 cup pancake batter
2 tbsp maple syrup
3 tbsp coconut sugar
2 tbsp cinnamon powder

Icing:

2 tbsp coconut condensed milk
2 tbsp plant milk
Or use maple butter

DIRECTIONS

1. In a bowl combine the wet ingredients, mix, then add the flour and mix well. Add the baking soda only when you're ready to cook. Otherwise the bubbles will deflate if you add it too early.

2. To make the cinnamon swirl combine 1/4 cup of the batter you just made and then the coconut sugar, maple syrup and cinnamon.

3. Preheat a skillet over medium heat and coat it with oil. If you're using a non stick skillet, then no oil is needed. Using a ¼ measuring cup, scoop pancake batter onto skillet. Starting at the center of the pancake add the cinnamon swirl in circles with a spoon or pour the filling to one corner of a sealable bag and pipe it.

4. Turn the pancake over, once the top starts to firm up. Fry the side with the swirl briefly (about 30 seconds).

5. To make the icing, mix together coconut condensed milk and and plant milk to loosen up the consistency. Drizzle over with a spoon and serve while warm!

Notes And Suggestions

You can use any gluten free flour blend you like, just make sure the batter is not too thin or too thick. The swirl should be slightly thicker and don't place it too close to the edge or it will go over the edges.

Ensure your skillet is hot before you start cooking. Keep the stove top temperature control knob at 3.

The pancakes are freezer friendly, keep in a sealed bag.

Serving size: 2 pancakes (without Icing): Calories: 252.2; Total Fat: 3.3 g; Total carbohydrate: 51.2 g; Protein: 5.3 g; Sugars: 13.5 g; Vitamin A: 3.9 %; Vitamin C: 1.3 %; Iron: 11.1 %; Calcium: 8.3 %.

Avocado Toast With Sardines

Savory avocado toast, featuring avocado, sardines, fresh onion and seeds on a crunchy toasted gluten free bread bun. So easy and perfect for those seeking a protein rich breakfast or snack.

Course: Breakfast   Makes 4 toasts   Ready in 7 minutes   GF, DF

INGREDIENTS

2 bread buns (see page 256), sliced in half
1 ripe avocado
4 red onion rings
4 oz wild sardines, packed in olive oil or water
a lemon wedge, the juice
pinch of Himalayan pink salt
pinch of black pepper
1 tbsp hemp seeds, to sprinkle

DIRECTIONS

1. Prepare your gluten free bread buns (pop them in the toaster).

2. Mash the avocado on top with a fork. Add the onion rings.

3. Sprinkle salt and black pepper, top with sardines and finish with hemp seeds or any other seeds you like. Squeeze some lemon juice on top for some sourness.

Notes And Suggestions

You can swap the sardines for smoked salmon, tuna, egg, roasted vegetables, pickles or even add some greens

As a bun you can also use a rice cake.

Once prepared the avocado toast is best consumed immediately since the avocado browns quickly.

Serving size: 2 toasts: Calories: 482.1; Total Fat: 26.8 g; Total carbohydrate: 44.9 g; Protein: 18.2 g; Sugars: 2 g; Vitamin A: 6.6 % Vitamin B-6: 24.1 %; Vitamin C: 12.7 %; Calcium: 23.3 %; Iron: 24.5 %; Magnesium 26.9 %; Zinc: 14.6 %.

Paleo Blueberry Banana Muffins

These healthy blueberry banana muffins are moist inside and with a crunchy cinnamon crumb topping. They can be made with fresh or frozen blueberries and are kid friendly. Perfect for a make ahead breakfast, dessert or mid morning snack.

Course: Breakfast   Makes 9 muffins   Ready in 40 minutes   GF, DF, P

INGREDIENTS

Batter

2 ripe mashed bananas
2 eggs (large)
1/3 cup plant milk
1/4 cup vegan butter, melted
(I used Miyoko's) or use oil
1/3 cup maple sugar
1 tbsp vanilla extract
1 tsp baking soda
1 tsp apple cider vinegar
pinch of salt
2 tbsp flax meal (ground flax seeds)
1 ⅔ cups gluten and grain free flour mix (see page 278)
1 cup frozen or fresh blueberries

Streusel (crumbly topping)

1/3 cup walnuts (chopped)
2 tbsp almond flour
2 tbsp maple sugar (or coconut sugar)
1/2 tsp cinnamon powder
1 Tbsp vegan butter (melted)

DIRECTIONS

1. Preheat oven to 360F (182C). In a bowl combine the mashed bananas with eggs, plant milk, melted vegan butter, sugar, vanilla extract, apple cider vinegar and mix well.

2. In another bowl sift together the flour, flax meal, salt and baking soda. Add the frozen blueberries, fold gently with a spatula until evenly coated with flour. This will prevent the batter from turning purple. Then mix the wet batter with the dry ingredients (do not overmix stir just until flour disappears). If you have fresh fruits just mix everything together in one bowl.

3. To make the streusel combine all ingredients in a small bowl and set aside.

4. Line a muffin pan with paper muffin cups. Spoon the batter into cups. Top each with streusel, gently pressing it down into the surface so it sticks; You can also add a couple of blueberries on top if you want them to be visible.

5. Bake the muffins for 30-35 minutes or until the muffin tops are golden brown

6. Remove the muffins from the oven, loosen their edges from the pan, and after about 5 minutes transfer them to a rack to cool.

Notes And Suggestions

You can easily replace the blueberries with other kind of fresh fruit, such as raspberries or peaches (chopped into small pieces).

For prettier muffins use wild blueberries, they are much smaller.

Serving size: **1 muffin:** Calories: 231.5 g; Total Fat: 14.4 g; Total carbohydrate: 26.6 g; Protein: 4.8 g; Sugars: 7.7 g; Fiber: 3.5 g; Vitamin A: 2.3 %; Vitamin C: 4.8 %; Iron: 4.9 %; Calcium: 4.8 %; Vitamin E: 11.4%

Basic French Crepes

Basic gluten and dairy free crepes - flexible, delicious, and versatile - a sweet or savory option for breakfast, brunch, lunch, dinner or dessert. The batter is easily made in a blender.

Course: Breakfast   Makes 12 crepes   Makes 12 crepes   GF, DF

INGREDIENTS

2 large eggs
2 cups non-dairy milk
3 tbsp oil or vegan butter
(melted)
1 ½ cups lightweight flour mix
(see page 272)
2 tbsp maple sugar or syrup
1 tsp vanilla extract
pinch of salt

DIRECTIONS

1. Add all ingredients in a blender and blend a few seconds until everything is nice and smooth. If you don't have a blender use a whisk or a hand mixer.

2. Cover the batter and let it rest for at least 20 minutes. The batter can be kept in the fridge overnight as well.

3. Preheat a 10 inch non-stick pan over medium heat. When the pan is hot, brush the surface with oil. If it's a ceramic non stick pan you don't need to grease it.

4. Mix the batter before you make each crepe to avoid any sediment. Pour 1/4 cup of the batter into the hot pan, and swirl to coat the the pan. Let the crepe cook about 50 seconds (until the edges are starting to brown), flip over the crepe gently, and cook for about 30 seconds on the other side.

5. Repeat until all the batter is used up. Stack the cooked crepes on a plate and cover with a lid or towel after each crepe you add (this will seal moisture and keep them nice and soft).

Notes And Suggestions

Resting the batter for 20 – 30 min. before cooking helps to dissolve and incorporate the batter ingredients better.

A non-stick pan is the best option for making crepes. The oil (or melted butter) added to batter will make the crepes more softer.

Keep the crepes in the fridge for up to 3 days or freeze them for up to 2 months.

Serving size: 1 crepe: Calories: 114.4; Total Fat: 4.7 g; Total carbohydrate: 15.4 g; Protein: 2.6 g; Sugars: 1.5 g; Vitamin A: 2.7% Vitamin B-12: 4.7 %; Vitamin D: 5%; Iron: 3.8 %; Calcium: 7.1 % .

Grain Free Banana Pancakes

Flourless banana pancakes with a very smooth and fluffy texture that almost melts in your mouth. There is no overpowering banana taste, enjoy them just like regular pancakes.

Course: Breakfast   Makes 14 pancakes   Ready in 1 hour 20 min   GF, DF, P

INGREDIENTS

2 large bananas
2 large eggs
1/2 cup plant yogurt
1/2 cup green banana flour
1/2 cup tigernut flour (or almond flour)
1 tsp vanilla extract
3/4 tsp baking soda
1 tsp apple cider vinegar or lemon juice
1 tsp cinnamon
pinch of salt
pinch of stevia extract powder for sweetness or your favorite sugar

Serve with:

plant based yogurt
fresh fruits (pear and kiwi)
honey or maple syrup

DIRECTIONS

1. Add all ingredients besides baking soda and apple cider vinegar, to a blender. Blend for several seconds until smooth. Then add those two and gently mix to combine.

2. Warm up a pan on low to medium heat. I noticed they tend to brown more rapidly than regular pancakes so make sure the temperature is set to the lower side.

3. Pour the batter in the pan, cooking about 3 medium pancakes at a time. Cook until bubbles start to form and the edges turn darker, then flip and cook for 1-2 additional minutes.

4. Repeat with the remaining batter until you have cooked all your pancakes.

Notes And Suggestions

Green banana flour is very neutral flavored and makes it suitable for many purposes. It has a slightly dark color but besides that it is comparable in taste and texture to wheat flour. But it absorbs more water: 3/4 cup of banana flour can be used in place of 1 cup of wheat flour in most recipes.

Use a non-stick skillet or griddle and you will not need any oil for frying.

Sprinkle chocolate chips, blueberries into mixture while cooking the first side.

Serving size: 2 pancakes: Calories: 112.1; Total Fat: 2.7 g; Total carbohydrate: 20.1 g; Fiber: 2.5 g; Protein: 2.3 g; Sugars: 6.8 g Vitamin A: 2.1 %; Vitamin C: 5.9 %; Vitamin B-12: 2 %; Vitamin B-6: 10.9 %; Iron: 2.2 %; Calcium: 1.1 %.

Oatmeal Superfood Breakfast

Enjoy the taste of oatmeal transformed into an extraordinary superfood breakfast with fresh fruit, non dairy yogurt, healthy fats and plant based protein. It's totally customizable so you can change and choose what toppings you want to add.

Course: Breakfast   Makes 1 serving   Ready in 15 min   GF, DF, V

INGREDIENTS

2/3 cup rolled oats (gluten free)
1 ⅓ cup plant milk (your choice)
salt to taste

Serve with:

plant milk yogurt (like coconut yogurt)
fresh blackberries (or other berries)
chia seeds
pumpkin seeds
hemp seed butter (or a nut butter)
honey or maple syrup drizzle (optional)

DIRECTIONS

1. Cook the oatmeal. Combine oats, water and salt in a medium saucepan. Bring to a boil, then reduce heat to low. Simmer uncovered for 3 to 5 minutes until thickened, stirring occasionally. Remove from heat and let cool slightly.

2. Assemble. Spoon the porridge on a plate or bowl, add 3-4 tbsp of dairy free yogurt and top with fresh berries and seeds. For protein and healthy fats, drizzle some hemp seeds butter or your favorite nut butter. Add honey, maple syrup (or maple butter) if you prefer it sweeter.

Notes And Suggestions

Cook the oatmeal the day before if you don't have time in the morning.

If you like some vanilla extract: this should be added just after cooking

You can also try some granola (see page 8) as topping for more crunchiness

Serving size: 1 bowl: Calories: 731.2; Total Fat: 38.2 g; Total carbohydrate: 71.8 g; Fiber: 17.5 g; Protein: 26.7 g; Sugars: 9.8 g Vitamin A: 13.6 %; Vitamin C: 37.8 %; Vitamin B-6: 7.5 %; Iron: 49.3%; Calcium: 28.5%; Vitamin E: 53.8%.

Veggie Fritters

Vegetable fritters that are crispy and golden brown on the outside, soft and creamy on the inside, and perfect with your favorite dip as breakfast or side dish. These fritters keep well, either chilled in the fridge or frozen in a sealed package for months.

Course: Breakfast   Makes 9 fritters   Ready in 35 min   GF, DF, P, W30

INGREDIENTS

3-4 cauliflower florets, grated
1 large zucchini, grated
2 medium potatoes, grated
3 eggs, lightly beaten
1-2 garlic cloves, minced
1/2 small onion, minced
1/2 cup cassava flour or other grain free flour
1 tsp Celtic sea salt
black pepper to taste

DIRECTIONS

1. In a large bowl finely shred the veggies with a hand grater.

2. With a muslin cloth squeeze the shredded veggies to remove the juices.

3. Once nice and dry, mix in the eggs, flour, minced onion and garlic plus seasonings. Mix to combine.

4. Heat olive oil in a large skillet over medium high heat. Scoop two tablespoons of batter for each fritter, flattening with a spatula, and cook on each side until is nicely golden brown, about 1-2 minutes. To cook without oil use a ceramic non stick skillet.

Notes And Suggestions

The secret of getting crisp edges is to squeeze out as much juice as possible after grating.

Add green onion or other veggies to the mix for more flavor.

Feel free to use other flour mixes.

Serving size: 1 fritter: Calories: 88.3; Total Fat: 1.8 g; Total carbohydrate: 14.7 g; Fiber: 2 g; Protein: 3.6 g; Sugars: 1.3 g; Vitamin A: 2 %; Vitamin C: 19.4 %; Vitamin B-6: 9.2 %; Iron: 3.6 %; Calcium: 1.5%; Magnesium: 3.7 %.

One Pan Meatless Cabbage Casserole

To make this casserole you need just one skillet. The cabbage is sauteed on stovetop, then baked in the oven along with other ingredients for a simple vegetarian breakfast or side dish.

Course: Breakfast   Makes 8 slices   Ready in 50 min   GF, DF

INGREDIENTS

6-7 cups shredded cabbage (packed)
1 large onion, chopped
3 garlic cloves
1 ½ cup plant milk
1 ¼ cup basmati rice, cooked
4 medium eggs
3-4 kale leaves, chopped
1/2 tsp turmeric powder
1/3 tsp coriander powder
1/2 tsp Himalayan pink salt
1/2 tsp black pepper
1/3 tsp mustard powder

DIRECTIONS

1. Shred the cabbage with a knife or a mandoline slicer (for thinner strips). You will need approximately 1/2 of a medium head of cabbage.

2. Chop the onion and the garlic cloves, saute until slightly golden then add the cabbage, salt, pepper, coriander, mustard powder and cook until it gets soft. Set aside.

3. In a bowl mix the eggs with salt and turmeric powder, then add the plant milk. Mix until well combined.

4. Divide the cabbage mixture into two portions, leaving half of it in the same skillet (I used a non-stick 10" ceramic skillet) add a thin layer of cooked rice, then kale and pour over half of the egg mixture. Repeat with another layer of cabbage, rice, kale and egg mixture. The liquid should cover slightly the surface for a perfect moist result.

5. Place the skillet in the preheated oven and bake at 380 F for 35-40 minutes until the surface is slightly golden.

6. When ready, cover with a heatproof cutting board and flip the skillet to release the content on the board. Cut and serve!

Notes And Suggestions

Feel free to use other veggies or even meat for a heartier meal.

Serving size: 1 slice: Calories: 122.7; Total Fat: 4.7 g; Total carbohydrate: 15.3 g; Fiber: 3.1 g; Protein: 6.4 g; Sugars: 3.9 g; Vitamin A: 71.5 %; Vitamin B-6: 9.2 %; Vitamin C: 61.1 %; Iron: 6.5 %; Calcium: 7.1 %; Magnesium: 4.7 %; Zinc: 3.7 %.

Breakfast Burrito

A gluten free breakfast wrap filled with scrambled eggs, chickpeas, lightly cooked veggies, and a creamy tangy chickpea sauce. It's easy to make and also a perfect make-ahead breakfast for days when you're short on time.

Course: Breakfast   Makes 4 burritos   Ready in 20 min   GF, DF

INGREDIENTS

4 gluten free tortillas (see recipe: page 244 or 248)

4 large eggs

1/2 cup cooked chickpeas

1/4 tsp salt

1/2 onion, finely chopped

2 stalks green onion, chopped

8 asparagus spears, trimmed

12 cherry tomatoes

1 bell pepper, chopped

1/4 cup chickpea sauce (see page 236) or any other sauce you like

DIRECTIONS

1. Prepare the eggs: Crack the eggs into a bowl, add salt, finely chopped onion and whisk them with a fork. In a skillet over medium heat, pour in the egg mixture and cook, stirring often, about 2 minutes. Transfer to a bowl.

2. In the same skillet add a bit of oil and once heated add the bell peppers, tomatoes, chickpeas cook for 2 minutes then add a bit of water and the asparagus, cover with a lid, reduce heat to low and let it steam for 2 minutes.

3. Assemble the burrito: Working with one tortilla at a time, spread about ⅓ cup cooked veggies on a tortilla about one-third from the edge. Drizzle 1 tablespoon chickpea sauce on top. Top with about ⅓ cup scrambled eggs and add some green onion (or just eyeball the amounts). Roll up by first folding the tortilla over from the bottom then fold in the two sides. Put the burrito seam side down on a plate. Repeat with the remaining burritos.

4. Serve at room temperature or heat them in a skillet, your choice. Halve the burritos, or serve them whole. Alternatively, you can package and refrigerate these up to 3 days and reheat before serving.

Notes And Suggestions

Feel free to use other veggies or even meat (replace the chickpeas) for a heartier meal. You can also add some avocado and salsa as well.

Serving size: 1 burrito: Calories: 217.7; Total Fat: 8.2 g; Total carbohydrate: 25.5 g; Fiber: 5 g; Protein: 10.9 g; Sugars: 5.2 g; Vitamin A: 22.7 %; Vitamin B-6: 18 %; Vitamin C: 78.4 %; Iron: 8.6 %; Calcium: 6.8 %; Magnesium: 10 %; Zinc: 7.1 %.

Fluffy Sourdough Pancakes

The fluffiest gluten free pancakes you can make with a gluten free sourdough starter. I make this recipe whenever I have a lot of sourdough discard. You can mix up the batter immediately in the morning, or the night before, and just add the baking soda and lemon juice before cooking.

Course: Breakfast   Makes 20-22 pancakes   Ready in 40 minutes   GF, DF

INGREDIENTS

3 medium-small bananas
3 medium eggs
1 ½ cups sourdough starter
1 cup oat flour
¼ cup maple syrup, or sugar
3 tbsp vegan butter, melted
¼ tsp salt
1 tsp baking soda
1 tsp lemon juice
1 tsp vanilla extract (optional)
1/3 cup non-dairy milk, to thin out; add more for thinner pancakes

Serve with:

fresh fruits
maple butter or syrup
nut butter or seed butter

DIRECTIONS

1. Mix bananas and eggs with a hand held blender until blended, then add the rest of ingredients besides baking soda and lemon juice. Mix again until smooth. Then add those two and gently mix just to combine and the batter puffs up.

2. Warm up a pan on low to medium heat. If you have a non-stick skillet you don't have to use oil for frying. Otherwise just use a touch before each round of pancakes.

3. Pour the batter in the pan, cooking about 3 medium pancakes at a time, or up to 5 smaller. Cook until bubbles start to form then flip and cook for 1 additional minute.

4. Repeat with the remaining batter until you have cooked all your pancakes.

Notes And Suggestions

If you can't have oats, use sorghum flour, buckwheat flour or use your favorite flour blend: the lightweight flour blend (see page 272), or other blend from the book.

This is a basic recipe but you can change the flavors as you like: sprinkle seeds, fruits, cinnamon, cacao powder on them while cooking on the first side.

Use 2 skillets simultaneously to cook them faster.

Serving size: 2 pancakes: Calories: 201.9; Total Fat: 4.9 g; Total carbohydrate: 33.4 g; Fiber: 2.2 g; Protein: 4.8 g; Sugars: 8.1 g, Vitamin A: 2.1 %; Vitamin C: 4.5 %; Vitamin B-12: 2.2 %; Vitamin B-6: 17 %; Iron: 4.7 %; Calcium: 5.9 %; Magnesium: 20.3 %.

Appetizers And Sides

Your get-together doesn't need to drip in cheap fat, processed carbs and added sugar. These gluten free dairy free appetizers and side dishes can be served for any occasion including parties and even larger crowds. Your guests will not even realize they are eating "health" food. In addition, use the recipes from bread and salad section to make healthy sliders or crostini.

Grilled Eggplant Rolls

Grilled eggplant slices filled with a salty, tangy, garlicky sauce, walnuts and tomato slices. An elegant yet easy appetizer perfect to impress a large crowd. You can also use pesto, herbs or mayo as your sauce, the combinations are endless.

Course: Appetizer   Makes 20 rolls   Ready in 1 hour 10 min   GF, DF, V, P, W30

INGREDIENTS

2 medium eggplants (cut into thin slices)
4 tbsp avocado oil (for grilling)
1 cup ranch dressing (see page 226)
1 garlic clove, finely minced
1/3 cup walnuts (minced)
4-5 medium tomatoes cut into strips (or bell peppers)

DIRECTIONS

1. Preheat your grill to high heat (if indoors, a stovetop grill pan will work). No need to spray the grill with oil.

2. Cut the eggplant lengthwise into really thin slices (about 20-24 total) and brush lightly each one with oil on both sides before placing on the grill. Grill in batches until softened, about 2 minutes each side. Sprinkle some salt on each one while removing from grill.

3. While the eggplant is cooling, in a small bowl, mix the pre-made ranch dressing, the extra clove of garlic and walnuts.

4. Spread a teaspoon of the mixture evenly over each eggplant slice and top with a strip of tomato or bell pepper. Carefully roll up the eggplant slices and place on a plate seam-side down. Garnish with some microgreens.

5. Refrigerate until ready to be served. The next day they are still good, but they tend to get a little soggy with time.

Notes And Suggestions

Eggplant slices should be thick and sturdy enough to hold together yet thin enough to roll up once cooked (a little less than 1/4 inch).

Feel free to experiment with fillings: you can use rice, bacon, pesto, cheese, avocado, cucumbers, the possibilities are endless.

Serving size: 4 rolls: Calories: 287.4; Total Fat: 21.3 g; Total carbohydrate: 19.8 g; Protein: 5.2 g; Sugars: 8.6 g; Dietary Fiber: 7.3 g; Vitamin A: 16.2 %; Vitamin B-6: 14.9; Vitamin C: 23.4 %; Iron: 6.8 %; Calcium: 3.1 %; Magnesium: 13.5 %.

Beetroot Crackers

Simple healthy beet crackers made from scratch. A delicious way to increase your veggie intake and satisfy your snack cravings. Serve with a dip, soup, salad or by themselves. And don't worry you will not feel the taste of beets in them.

Course: Appetizer   Makes 40 crackers   Ready in 35 min   GF, DF, V

INGREDIENTS

1 cup pureed beets (steamed beets + 4 tbsp water)
1/2 cup flax seed meal
3/4 cup sorghum flour
1/4 cup arrowroot starch
2 tbsp chia seeds
2 tbsp black sesame seeds
1 tsp onion powder
1/4 tsp garlic powder
1/2 tsp paprika
1 tsp salt
4 tbsp avocado oil
Also see recipe video on the blog.

DIRECTIONS

1. Cut 1 large beetroot into quarters and place into the pot or steamer. Allow to steam for 15 minutes, or until they feel tender when pierced with a fork. Keep the water for later.

2. To a blender add the steamed beets, 4 tbsp of the water underneath the steamer (it still has some vitamins leaked in there). Add the oil and the flaxseed meal and blend until you get a smooth paste.

3. Transfer to a large bowl and mix the rest of ingredients to form a soft sticky dough. Let it rest for 10-15 minutes.

4. Preheat the oven to 375 F. Use half of the dough and roll out with a rolling pin between two parchment papers. The layer should be about 1/8 inch (3 mm) thick.

5. Remove the top paper and transfer on a cookie sheet and bake for 5-8 min. Then take it out and using a cookie cutter or a pizza cutter, form the shapes you want. It's easier to cut when the dough is more solid. Put it back in the oven for another 20 minutes (25 min total).

6. At this time the edges can be removed and if the ones in the middle are not done yet, close the oven door with the heat off and leave the crackers to harden and dry in the residual heat for about 30 minutes.

Notes And Suggestions

You can replace the sorghum flour with millet flour, buckwheat flour, oat flour or rice flour. For best results keep the ratio of whole grain flour and starch flour the same as specified in the recipe.

The use of oil is optional but it helps a lot in crispiness and prevents the dough from sticking to the paper.

Serving size: 4 crackers: Calories: 38.4; Total Fat: 2 g; Total carbohydrate: 4 g; Protein: 0.8 g; Sugars: 0.4 g; Dietary Fiber: 1.2 g; Vitamin A: 0.4 %; Vitamin C: 0.4 %; Iron: 1.6 %; Calcium: 0.8 %.

Roasted Red Pepper Hummus

Hummus made with roasted red bell peppers, chickpeas, tahini and spices. This hummus is creamy, smoky, slightly sweet and perfect for dipping crackers or fresh vegetables.

Course: Appetizer   Makes 2 ⅓ cups   Ready in 10 min   GF, DF, V

INGREDIENTS

1 ⅓ cup roasted red bell peppers (about 3 peppers)
2 cups cooked chickpeas, drained and rinsed
2 tbsp tahini paste
2 tbsp extra virgin olive oil
1 ½ tbsp fresh lemon juice
2 garlic cloves
1/2 teaspoon cumin
1/2 tsp smoked paprika
1/2 tsp salt (or more to taste)
ground black pepper (to taste)
1/4 tsp cayenne pepper (if you like it hot)
2-4 tbsp warm water (to thin it out)
dried parsley (to garnish)
crushed red chili peppers (to garnish)

DIRECTIONS

1. In a food processor, combine the chickpeas with the roasted red peppers, tahini, garlic and puree to a chunky paste.

2. Scrape down the side of the bowl. Add the lemon juice and the olive oil, the seasonings and puree until smooth.

3. With the machine running, slowly add water, one tablespoon at a time, until the hummus is creamy and smooth.

4. Scrape the hummus into a bowl. Drizzle with olive oil and sprinkle some dried parsley, crushed red chili peppers and serve with chips, crackers or raw vegetables.

Notes And Suggestions

Use jarred or freshly roasted red peppers, both work well.

The hummus will last for up to a week in the fridge, if kept in a sealed airtight container. Or freeze for up to 1 month.

If you don't like chickpeas, you can substitute those with white beans.

In the picture the hummus is served with beet crackers (page 54).

Serving size: 1/4 cup: Calories: 126.6; Total Fat: 6.4 g; Total carbohydrate: 14.1 g; Protein: 4.5 g; Sugars: 3 g; Dietary Fiber: 3.8 g; Vitamin A: 11.2%; Vitamin C: 29.4 %; Iron: 3.8 %; Calcium: 2.8 %.

Pineapple Avocado Salsa

A sweet and sour salsa to go with barbecue chicken, steak, fish, hamburgers, tacos or served with chips as a delicious side dish.

Course: Appetizer   Makes 2 ½ cups   Ready in 15 min   GF, DF, V, P, W30

INGREDIENTS

1 cup fresh pineapple, diced
1/2 red onion, diced
small bell pepper, diced
1 large avocado, diced
1/2 cup diced parsley leaves, or cilantro
3 tbsp fresh lime juice
salt and pepper to taste

DIRECTIONS

1. Combine all diced ingredients in a bowl and gently toss together, taking care not to mash the avocado. Squeeze the lime juice, season with salt and pepper according to your taste.

2. Allow to sit for 15 to 30 minutes before serving, so the flavors could meld better, then toss again.

Notes And Suggestions

Use 2 tbsp diced jalapeno peppers if you prefer it spicy.

I chose pineapple because it's rich in enzymes and is excellent when combined with other foods: aids the digestion and absorption of proteins. But you can choose other fruit like mango, peach or whatever is in season.

Aromatic herbs that go well besides cilantro and parsley: basil, marjoram, mint or tarragon.

The lime juice will keep the salsa fresh in the fridge and will prevent the avocado from turning brown. Place the salsa in an airtight container, it will last in the fridge for up to 24-36 hours.

Serving size: 1/2 cup: Calories: 87.9; Total Fat: 5.6 g; Total carbohydrate: 10 g; Protein: 1.6 g; Sugars: 3.8 g; Dietary Fiber: 4.2 g; Vitamin A: 13.2 %; Vitamin B-6: 8.3 %; Vitamin C: 53.8 %; Iron: 4.4 %; Calcium: 1.8 %; Magnesium: 4.4%.

Roasted Shitake Mushrooms

These oven roasted shiitake mushrooms are a great addition to any meal, they can be served with rice, quinoa, buckwheat or even along with a salad for boosting it's flavor.

Course: Appetizer   Makes 4 cups   Ready in 30 min   GF, DF, V, P, W30

INGREDIENTS

30 shiitake mushrooms
5 tbsp extra virgin olive oil
1/3 tsp ground black pepper
3 garlic cloves, finely minced
1 tsp rosemary, dry or fresh
1/2 tsp thyme, dry or fresh
2 tbsp lemon juice (or apple cider vinegar)
1/3 tsp Celtic sea salt
2 tbsp parsley leaves, chopped, to garnish.

DIRECTIONS

1. Heat the oven to 400°F. Line a large baking sheet with parchment paper.

2. Lightly wipe the mushrooms of dirt and soil. Trim tough stems (leave the soft ones). Slice the mushrooms into strips, 1/2" thick.

3. In a large bowl mix together everything except the mushrooms (to form a marinade) then toss in the mushrooms and make sure they are all well coated. Place in one layer on the baking sheet.

4. Roast for 10 minutes, then toss the mushrooms once, and return to the oven. Roast for additional 10-15 minutes.

5. Then transfer to a serving dish and top with chopped parsley. Serve immediately.

Notes And Suggestions

If you don't have shiitake mushrooms, use any kind of mushrooms you like, or combine 2-3 types.

For extra flavor drizzle a little coconut aminos as a soy sauce substitute.

Serving size: 1 cup: Calories: 231.3; Total Fat: 6.4 g; Total carbohydrate: 17.9 g; Protein: 2.4 g; Sugars: 5.2 g; Dietary Fiber: 3.4 g; Vitamin A: 3.5 %; Vitamin C: 6.5 %; Iron: 5.9 %; Calcium: 1.8 %; Selenium: 48.3 %; Copper: 61.1 %.

Herring Forshmak

An old classic appetizer from Eastern European cuisine that can be made in multiple variations. The brined herring gives it a salty tangy fishy flavor that blends very well with the rest of more mild tasting ingredients. It's usually served with bread, crackers or crudités.

Course: Appetizer   Makes 3 cups   Ready in 20 min   GF, DF

INGREDIENTS

5-6 oz wild caught herring fillet (pickled)
2 hard boiled eggs
5 tbsp dairy free butter, room temperature
1 medium onion, diced
1 tsp Dijon mustard
2-3 slices of gluten free bread (I used my gluten free sourdough bread)
1/4 tsp ground cumin
1/2 tsp ground coriander
salt and pepper to taste

DIRECTIONS

1. In a hot skillet with oil sauté the diced onion until golden.
Prepare the herring fillet by removing any bones and peeling the thin layer of skin.

2. Using a food processor roughly mix all the ingredients but be careful, do not overmix the texture should be a little chunky. Alternatively you can chop everything very finely. If the result is too dry, add 1-2 tbsp plant based milk. If it's too wet add more bread.

3. Place in the refrigerator for at least 1 hour to harden.

4. Sprinkle with chopped pecans, sesame seeds and some microgreens or scallions. Serve with your favorite gluten free bread, crackers or crudités

Notes And Suggestions

Keep refrigerated for up to a week.

Some people prefer to add grated apples or cooked potatoes.

If you can't find the herring, you can use any fish, like anchovies or sardines.

Serving size: 1/2 cup: Calories: 186.9; Total Fat: 8.6 g; Total carbohydrate: 7.5 g; Protein: 6.1 g; Sugars: 3.5 g; Dietary Fiber: 0.7 g; Vitamin A: 6 %; Vitamin B-12: 19.9 %; Vitamin C: 2.9 %; Iron: 3.6 %; Calcium: 3.3 %; Vitamin D: 40.3 %; Selenium: 27.3 %.

Savory Crepe Pockets

Savory French crepes filled with a mixture of ground beef, mushrooms and served with a drizzle of creamy avocado sauce. This makes an absolutely finger licking amazing appetizer, side dish, or even a meal.

Course: Appetizer   Makes 10 stuffed crepes   Ready in 20 min   GF, DF

INGREDIENTS

10 crepes (see page 36)

Filling:

1/2 pound ground beef
6-7 mini portobello mushrooms, finely chopped
1 small onion, finely chopped
1 medium carrot finely chopped or grated
1/2 tsp coriander powder
1/2 tsp paprika
1/4 tsp curry (optional)
salt & pepper, to taste
2 tbsp extra virgin olive oil, for sautéing

Avocado sauce:

1 large avocado, ripe
2 scallion stalks
handful of parsley
juice of half a lime
1/2 tsp Himalayan pink salt
1 tbsp coconut aminos
2 tbsp filtered water

DIRECTIONS

1. Make the filling. In a hot skillet with oil, sauté chopped onion and carrots for 2 minutes, then add the mushrooms, stir and saute for another 3-4 minutes.

Add the ground beef with all seasonings, stir and cook until the meat is done. Let it cool before assembling the crepes. You can make it the day before if you like.

2. Assemble the crepes. Take a crepe and place about 2 tbsp of the filling 1 inch from the bottom edge and fold it up on top of the filling, then fold in the two sides. Roll the crepe just like blintzes (or burrito) with the seam facing down. Repeat with remaining crepes.

Then add them to a non stick skillet over medium heat with a drizzle of oil. Cook for 2 minutes per side, or until golden and crisp. Do this in batches.

3. Make the sauce. Place all ingredients in a blender and mix until smooth.

Transfer the stuffed crepes to a plate, top with a drizzle of avocado sauce and sprinkle some greens. Serve!

Notes And Suggestions

As alternative filling you can also use shredded chicken, fish or some sautéed vegetables and serve them with a salad for dinner. Some people prefer to add boiled eggs to the filling.

Serving size: **1 stuffed crepe:** Calories: 218.4; Total Fat: 11.2 g; Total carbohydrate: 19.7 g; Protein: 12.1 g; Sugars: 1.2 g; Dietary Fiber: 2.3 g; Vitamin A: 29.8 %; Vitamin B-12: 2.1 %; Vitamin C: 2.5 %; Iron: 11.6 %; Calcium: 5.3 %; Vitamin D: 5.9 %.

Roasted Potato Strips

Roasted potato and sweet potato strips - a healthy alternative to French fries. This baking method allows you to keep the fat to a minimum by tossing the potatoes in just enough oil to give them flavor and a crispy crust. Pairs well with almost any main dish you are serving.

Course: Appetizer   Makes 4 servings   Ready in 50 min   GF, DF, V, P, W30

INGREDIENTS

2 large russet potatoes
2 large sweet potatoes
2 tbsp extra virgin olive oil
2 tbsp adobo seasoning
(to make your own, combine:
1/2 tsp garlic powder
1/2 tsp onion powder
1 tsp sea salt
1/3 tsp black pepper
1/4 tsp oregano
1/4 tsp ground bay leaf and 1/4
tsp ground turmeric or paprika)

DIRECTIONS

1. Preheat the oven to 420°F.

2. Peel and cut the potatoes lengthwise into strips 1/2 inch thick, 1/2 inch wide.

3. Place the potatoes in a bowl. Drizzle with the olive oil and seasonings and toss to coat evenly.

4. Preheat a baking sheet in the oven for 5 minutes. Remove from the oven, cover with parchment paper and carefully arrange the potatoes in a single layer on the hot baking sheet.

5. Roast the potatoes for 40 minutes, lowering the temperature to 400F after 20 minutes until golden brown.

Notes And Suggestions

Use white potatoes, sweet potatoes, carrots, parsnips or any other root vegetable you like.

Serving size: 10 strips: Calories: 181.5; Total Fat: 5.4 g; Total carbohydrate: 31.8 g; Protein: 3 g; Sugars: 3.3 g; Dietary Fiber: 3.3 g; Vitamin A: 261 %; Vitamin B-6: 15.2%; Vitamin C: 51.6 %; Iron: 6.5 %; Calcium: 3 %.

White Bean Dip With Caramelized Onions

A creamy white bean dip topped with sweet caramelized onions. This is a simple dish that can be served as a dip with chips and raw veggies, as a spread, as an appetizer or side dish.

Course: Appetizer   Makes 2 servings   Ready 1h 50 min   GF, DF, V

INGREDIENTS

2 cups white beans (navy) cooked
2 large white onions, diced
3 tbsp avocado oil (or olive oil)
5-6 medium garlic cloves, minced
1 tsp sea salt
1/3 tsp freshly ground black pepper
2 bay leaves
1 tsp cumin powder
1 tsp paprika (use smoked paprika for more flavor)

DIRECTIONS

1. Soak and cook the beans. Soak overnight in cool water (at least 8 hours). In the morning drain the beans and transfer to a pot and cover with twice as much water. Bring to a boil over medium heat then reduce to low and simmer, uncovered, until the beans start to become tender. Season with salt and pepper.

2. Caramelize the onions. While the beans are cooking, heat the oil in a large pan over medium heat. Add the diced onions, let them soften for 3-4 minutes then add the minced garlic, seasonings, bay leaves and reduce the heat to low. Cook, stirring occasionally, until the onions are golden and caramelized, 15 to 20 minutes. Remove the bay leaves.

3. Assemble. Remove the beans (drained) and place in a blender along with half of the caramelized onions. To help blending add a few tbsp of liquid from beans or some vegetable stock. Ladle the bean puree into a serving dish. Top with the rest of caramelized onions, some freshly ground pepper and a drizzle of coconut aminos (optional).

Notes And Suggestions

Use any white beans: Navy, Cannellini or Baby Lima Beans. Use canned beans for faster results.

Add 1-2 tbsp of balsamic vinegar in the caramelized onion if you don't have coconut aminos. Sprinkle some toasted nuts (optional). Serve with pickled vegetables, gluten free bread or crackers.

Serving size: half of mixture: Calories: 475.9; Total Fat: 20.7 g; Total carbohydrate: 53.6 g; Protein: 15.7 g; Sugars: 7 g; Dietary Fiber: 13.6 g; Vitamin A: 11.7 %; Vitamin B-6: 16.5%; Vitamin C: 22.6 %; Iron: 8.8 %; Calcium: 6 %; Magnesium: 10.1 %.

Baked Ranch Chicken Wings

Crispy oven baked chicken wings doused in a creamy dairy free ranch sauce, and yes, you can totally get that crispiness without having to fry them. These wings make an excellent weeknight appetizer, side dish or an easy game-day dish.

Course: Appetizer   Makes 4 servings   Ready in 50 min   GF, DF, P, W30

INGREDIENTS

2 lb chicken wings
3 tbsp avocado oil
6 tbsp ranch dressing (see page 226)
1/2 tsp additional salt

DIRECTIONS

1. Heat oven to 425 F. Line a large pan or two smaller with parchment paper.

2. In large bowl, add chicken wings, oil, stir in ranch dressing and some additional salt (because this homemade dressing doesn't have a lot of salt) toss to coat evenly.

3. Spread wings in pans in a single layer. Make sure they are not touching if you want a crust on all sides.

4. Bake 20 minutes. Remove from oven, and turn wings over. Return to oven, rotate pans, and continue baking another 15-20 minutes or until a nice brown crust is formed.

Notes and Suggestions

For best results, it's best to leave the chicken wings to marinate (in the ranch sauce) for a couple of hours before baking, or even overnight. But you can do it right away as well with wonderful results.

Serving size: 5 wings: Calories: 320; Total Fat: 20.2 g; Total carbohydrate: 7.2 g; Protein: 26.4 g; Sugars: 4.1 g; Dietary Fiber: 0.8 g; Vitamin A: 4.5 %; Vitamin B-6: 19.4 %; Vitamin B-12: 5%; Vitamin C: 8.5 %; Iron: 7.9 %; Calcium: 4 %.

Green Bean, Potato & Mushroom Medley

An easy dish packed with flavor prepared mainly due to steam without involving frying or the need of oil. This can be served as a side dish or as a meal and it tastes even better as warmed up leftovers the next day. If you prefer a non-vegan dish you can also add some bacon too.

Course: Appetizer   Makes 4 servings   Ready in 30 min   GF, DF, V, W30

INGREDIENTS

6 oz fresh green beans (wax beans will work too)
6 large golden Yukon potatoes, cubed
4 oz baby bella mushrooms, sliced
4-5 garlic cloves, finely minced
1 large white onion, finely chopped
2 bay leaves
3/4 cup water or vegetable stock
1 tsp sea salt, or to taste
Black pepper to taste chopped parsley, scallions or dill, to garnish

DIRECTIONS

1. In a deep pan, add the stock or water bring to a boil then add the potatoes and the bay leaves. Cover the pan tightly with a lid and cook over low heat for 15 minutes.

2. Then add the onion, green beans and mushrooms, give it a stir, cook more until everything is tender.

3. At the end add the minced garlic, salt and pepper to taste and simmer for another 4-5 minutes, the liquid will be almost gone.

4. Transfer in a dip dish and garnish with chopped greens. Serve!

Notes and Suggestions

If you want more flavor and don't mind about using oil in your dish, try to caramelize the onions and the mushrooms in a skillet then add those at the end with garlic.

1-2 tablespoons of vegan butter would be a great addition too.

Serving size: ~ 2 cups: Calories: 192.2; Total Fat: 0.1 g; Total carbohydrate: 48.1 g; Protein: 8.3 g; Sugars: 8.3 g; Dietary Fiber: 7.1 g; Vitamin A: 8.6 %; Vitamin B-12: 5%; Vitamin C: 86.5 %; Iron: 13.9 %; Calcium: 5.8 %; Magnesium: 14.7 %.

73

Roasted Eggplant Dip

A Middle Eastern eggplant dip known as baba ganoush but tweaked to be more flavorful with lots of texture but still soft and silky! Great to serve with crackers or bread, as an appetizer or side dish.

Course: Appetizer   Makes 3 cups   Ready in 1h 10 min   GF, DF, V, P, W30

INGREDIENTS

2 large eggplants
1 large onion, chopped
4 garlic cloves, minced
3 tbsp olive oil
3/4 cup walnut halves
1/4 cup parsley leaves, minced
1/4 cup lemon juice, fresh
1 tsp Celtic sea salt, or to taste
black pepper to taste

DIRECTIONS

1. Preheat oven to 400 degrees F. Cut the eggplants in halves and sprinkle generously with salt. Allow the eggplant to rest for 10-15 minutes to release some water. Then use a paper towel to wipe away as much moisture and salt as possible.

2. Transfer to the prepared baking sheet, flesh-side-down and roast in the oven for 45-50 minutes, until they are tender and have started to collapse.

3. Remove from oven and allow to cool enough to handle, then use a spoon to scoop out the meat. Place in a colander to drain for 15 minutes, this will get rid of the excess water.

4. Meanwhile heat a skillet on the stove top with olive oil and sauté the chopped garlic and onion until slightly golden. Or use them raw if you like.

5. Transfer to a food processor, add the walnuts, parsley and pulse a few times, then add the drained eggplant, salt and lemon juice. Pulse a couple of times just to mix it. Chill for one hour, sprinkle with parsley before serving.

Notes and Suggestions

Use other nuts or seeds as walnut replacement.

If you don't have lemon juice, apple cider vinegar or balsamic vinegar works too.

Serving size: 1/3 cup: Calories: 146.6; Total Fat: 11.2 g; Total carbohydrate: 11.8 g; Protein: 3.1 g; Sugars: 5.6 g; Dietary Fiber: 4.3 g; Vitamin A: 5.1 %; Vitamin B-6: 10.2 %; Vitamin C: 14 %; Calcium: 3 %; Iron: 4.4 %; Magnesium: 9.7 %; Zinc: 3.5%.

Main Dishes

••

This section includes main dishes and entrées made from scratch with whole clean foods, without any processed ingredients, suitable for dinner or lunch. From quick and easy to make-ahead, from vegan to paleo, these recipes are all perfect for a family dinner during a busy weeknight or for larger holiday gatherings.

Teriyaki Turkey Tenderloins & Green Salad

Turkey tenderloins marinated in a delicious teriyaki sauce (whole30 approved) served with a green salad and finished with a simple fresh lemon dressing.

Course: Main   Serves 2 people   Ready in 35 minutes   GF, DF, P, W30

INGREDIENTS

2 turkey tenderloins

Teriyaki sauce:
5 large prunes
3 tbsp balsamic vinegar
1 tbsp olive oil
5 tbsp water
1/2 tsp salt
1 tsp paprika
1/2 inch fresh ginger
3 garlic cloves, minced
1 tsp onion powder

Salad:

1 ½ cup Tuscan kale, chopped
1 ½ cup lettuce, shredded
handful of chopped parsley
1 large cucumber, spiralized
1 medium sweet potato, cubed
and roasted
1 ½ avocado, cubed

Salad dressing:

3 tsp lemon juice
1 tbsp olive oil
salt and pepper to taste

DIRECTIONS

1. Place the turkey tenderloins in a bowl and set aside.

2. In a blender combine all the ingredients for the teriyaki sauce, blend until smooth, add a little more water if it's too thick. Pour half of the sauce over turkey and shake to coat. Marinate in the refrigerator for 1 to 3 hours.

3. Preheat oven at 425 F. Remove turkey from the marinade and place on a heated grill pan. Turn down the oven to 400F and bake for 25 minutes total, turning once and brushing with the rest of the marinade halfway through cooking.

4. Cut the sweet potato into cubes and place in the bowl in which the turkey was marinated, shake to coat and bake at the same time with the meat on a separate sheet.

5. While the turkey and potatoes are roasting, prepare the salad: chop the greens, julienne or spiralize the cucumber and cube the avocados.

6. To prepare the salad dressing: mix all ingredients and pour over the salad just before serving.

Notes And Suggestions

The meat is cooked through when pierced with a fork the juices run clear.

Taste for dressing and salt and add more as needed.

Serving size: 1 turkey tenderloin: Calories: 561.1; Total Fat: 22.1 g; Sugar: 8.5 g; Total carbohydrate: 19.5 g; Protein: 69.3 g; Vitamin A: 14.4%; Vitamin C: 1.7 %; Iron: 35.7 %; Calcium: 7.3 %. **Serving size: half a salad**: Calories: 383.3; Total Fat: 27.3 g; Sugar: 3.9 g; Carbohydrates: 35.1 g; Protein: 6.1 g; Vitamin A: 450.3 %; Vitamin C: 176.8 %; Iron: 15.9 %; Calcium: 13.3 %.

Creamy Beef And Mushroom Stroganoff

Tender beef chunks and mushrooms in a creamy, silky sauce with a mild tangy taste. It comes together quickly especially if you have some leftover steak. Serve over veggies or your favorite cooked gluten free grains.

Course: Main   Serves 4 people   Ready in 35 minutes   GF, DF, P, W30

INGREDIENTS

1 lb steak tips, or sirloin or beef tenderloin, cut into cubes
3/4 tsp dried rosemary powder
3/4 tsp paprika
1/2 tsp Celtic sea salt
1/4 tsp black pepper
1 large onion, chopped
2 garlic cloves, grated
8 oz, sliced white mushrooms

The sauce:

1 ½ cup of water, warm
1/3 cup coconut cream
1 tbsp apple cider vinegar
3 tbsp vegan butter
2 tbsp vegan cream cheese (I used Miyoko's)
3 tbsp coconut aminos
1 tsp Dijon mustard
2 tbsp arrowroot powder
salt to taste
Steamed cauliflower and roasted potatoes for serving
(salad-optional)

DIRECTIONS

1. Toss the steak tips with the salt, ground black pepper, paprika and rosemary. Then add the chopped onions and garlic, give it a mix, set aside.

2. Add 1 tablespoon avocado oil to a large sauté pan over medium-high heat. Once hot, add the seasoned beef to the pan. Sear for 1-2 minutes, until browned and slightly caramelized. Then add the sliced mushrooms, cook for about 1 minute. Remove all from the pan and set aside.

3. In the same pan make the sauce. But first combine all ingredients (except the arrowroot powder and butter) in warm water to dissolve evenly). Add the butter to the pan and sprinkle the arrowroot powder and whisk to combine. Once smooth, pour in slowly the liquid mixed earlier, whisking constantly. Let the mixture come to a bubble then add back the beef and mushrooms.

4. Reduce the heat to low and taste for seasoning. Add salt if needed. Let cook for additional 2-3 minutes.

Remove from heat and serve over your favorite vegetables.

Notes And Suggestions

You can also serve this over brown rice, cauliflower rice, buckwheat, zucchini noodles, inside a baked sweet potato, mashed, steamed or roasted vegetables.

Keep in the fridge for 3-4 days. To freeze, allow to cool completely and store in a container for up to 3 months. Thaw in the refrigerator overnight, then re-heat on medium-low until warmed through.

Serving size: 1.5 cup beef, mushrooms and sauce: Calories: 450.5; Total Fat: 30.3 g; Sugar: 8.8 g; Total carbohydrate: 15.5 g; Fiber: 1.6 g; Protein: 27.5 g; Vitamin A: 3%; Vitamin C: 6.1 %; Iron: 13.2 %; Calcium: 4.1 %; Selenium: 43.2 %; Zinc: 25.9 %.

Braised Oxtail

The long, slow cooking paired with aromatic vegetables releases the marrow and gelatin from the oxtail into a silky, nutrient dense sauce. This makes a flavorful rustic comfort food perfect for a wintery day.

Course: Main   Serves 3-4 people   Ready in 3 hours   GF, DF, P, W30

INGREDIENTS

1 tbsp olive oil, extra virgin (or avocado oil)
2 ½ pounds oxtails
1 large onion, chopped
2 stalks celery, chopped
4 garlic cloves, minced
2 carrots, chopped
2 white potatoes, peeled and cubed
1/2 jar diced tomatoes (about 8 ½ ounces)
2 ½ cup of water or stock
3/4 tsp Celtic sea salt
1/4 tsp ground black pepper
2 bay leaves
1 ½ tsp rosemary, or 2 fresh sprigs

DIRECTIONS

1. Season the oxtail with salt and black pepper. Set aside.

2. Preheat the oven to 325 degrees F. Heat the olive oil in a oven proof pot over medium heat on stove top. Brown the oxtail in batches on all sides.

3. In the same pot stir in the diced tomatoes, potatoes, water, rosemary and bay leaves. Season with salt and pepper and cook until it starts to simmer.

4. Cover with a lid and transfer the pot in the oven to simmer gently.

5. After 1.5 hours, in the same pot add onion, garlic, carrots and celery. Add more liquid (like stock or water) if it reduced. It should barely cover the meat.

6. Cover and return to oven for another hour or so. By delaying the addition of vegetables helps them preserve some of the vitamins. The long cooking usually reduces all the nutritional value of fresh vegetables.

7. When the oxtail is tender and the meat slips easily off the bone, then it's ready. Serve with rice, mashed potatoes, a green salad or any side you like!

Notes And Suggestions

The flavor improves as it sits. Because of the natural gelatin in the oxtail and cooked vegetables, you don't need to add any thickeners to the sauce.

Serving size: 1/4 of the portion: Calories: 1296.5; Total Fat: 123.8 g; Sugar: 6.7 g; Total carbohydrate: 26.6 g; Protein: 17.2 g; Vitamin A: 275.3 %; Vitamin B-6: 9.6 %; Vitamin B-12: 18 %; Vitamin C: 44 %; Iron: 11.8 %; Calcium: 6.4 %.

| Main Dishes

Savory Twice Baked Sweet Potatoes

This recipe is perfect as a main or side dish for your holiday table. These little vegan stuffed sweet potatoes deliver a savory combination of caramelized onions, brown rice, cranberry, pecans and bell peppers – all baked and finished with a balsamic maple glaze.

Course: Main   Serves 4 people   Ready in 1 h 20 minutes   GF, DF, V

INGREDIENTS

4 medium sweet potatoes
1 medium onion, diced
2 tbsp olive oil, extra virgin
1/2 red bell pepper, cubed
1/2 cup organic brown rice
(about 2/3 cup - cooked)
1/2 cup dried cranberries
1/3 cup chopped pecans, or walnuts
2 tbsp parsley, finely chopped, for garnish

Maple balsamic glaze:

4 tbsp olive oil, extra virgin
3 tbsp balsamic vinegar
2 large garlic cloves, minced
2 tbsp maple syrup
1 tsp stone ground brown mustard
dash of Himalayan pink salt
dash of cracked black pepper

DIRECTIONS

1. Preheat the oven to 400 degrees. Line a large baking tray with parchment paper. Use a fork to poke a couple holes in each sweet potato to prevent exploding. Bake for 45 minutes to 1 hour (depending on how large the sweet potatoes are).

2. While the sweet potatoes are roasting, boil the brown rice, let it cool.

3. Prepare the glaze: to a small container add all ingredients and mix to combine. Set aside.

4. In large pan over medium heat, sauté the onions in 2 tbsp of olive oil until golden. To the onion then add the bell peppers, chopped pecans (or walnuts), rinsed cranberries, and the cooled brown rice. Stir to combine and cook for 1-2 minutes. Toss half of the glaze on top of the cooking mixture. Taste and season with salt and pepper if needed and remove from heat.

5. Remove the sweet potatoes from the oven and let them cool for 10 minutes or until you can safely handle them. Cut in half (not all the way through) and carefully scoop out the insides (pulp) into a large bowl. Leave a thin layer of pulp to support the skin and serve as walls.

6. Add the pulp of the sweet potatoes into the rice mixture. (You can mash it or finely chop it). Then scoop the mixture back into the potato skins and put the tray back in the oven for 10 minutes to warm them up.

7. Remove the sweet potatoes from the oven, drizzle the rest of maple balsamic glaze over the top and garnish with freshly chopped parsley.

Serving size: 1 stuffed sweet potato: Calories: 436.8; Total Fat: 24.9 g; Sugar: 21.3 g; Total carbohydrate: 51.8 g; Protein: 4.6 g; Sodium: 81 mg; Fiber: 7 g; Vitamin A: 765 %; Vitamin C: 53.4 %; Iron: 2.1 %; Calcium: 66 %.

| Main Dishes

Easy Sauteed Sirloin Tips

Simple one skillet sirloin tips soaked in an aromatic marinade and combined with fresh vegetables. Serve with any side dish of your choice. Perfect for a quick weeknight dinner!

Course: Main　　　　Serves 2 people　　　　Ready in 30 minutes　　　GF, DF, P, W30

INGREDIENTS

1.4 pound beef sirloin tip steak, cut into strips

Marinade:

3 tbsp olive oil, extra virgin
3 tbsp vinegar (apple cider)
3 tbsp coconut aminos (as soy sauce substitute)
1 tsp Celtic sea salt
1 ½ tsp black pepper
1 tsp dried rosemary (powdered)
1 ½ tsp onion powder
4 fresh garlic cloves (finely minced)

Vegetables:

1 large sweet bell pepper, cut into strips
1 large carrot, chopped
3 stalks of green onion, chopped
4-5 large leaves of Tuscan kale, chopped

DIRECTIONS

1. Prepare and mix the marinade ingredients in a medium bowl. Cut the stake into thin strips (a little less than ½ inch thick) and mix with the marinade in the same bowl. Cover and keep in the fridge for at least 2 hours or overnight.

2. Sauté the meat. Heat 2 tablespoons of oil in the skillet on high heat, until the oil is really hot, but not smoking. Add the strips of beef in one layer (marinade discarded), let them brown initially, without stirring, then turn them over. Cook for no more than 2 minutes (for medium-rare) and 3-4 minutes total (for medium well). Repeat with the remaining beef. Remove the strips on a plate and keep warm.

3. Sauté the vegetables. In the same skillet add another tbsp of oil. Add the chopped onions, carrots and bell peppers, cook, stirring, until they start to get tender, about 5-8 minutes. Turn off the heat, add the beef strips and the chopped kale, give it a good stir and taste if any salt or pepper is needed.

Usually you don't need to add any seasoning, because some marinade leftovers will coat the vegetables as well. Serve immediately!

Notes And Suggestions

Marinating the thinly sliced steak will tenderize the meat while adding flavor and will make it less chewy. Bring to room temperature before cooking.

Serving size: half of skillet: Calories: 1005.2; Total Fat: 71.3; Sugar: 7.8 g; Total carbohydrate: 24.5 g; Protein: 64.3 g; Vitamin A: 439.3 %; Vitamin B-6: 21.6 %; Vitamin C: 239.7%; Iron: 11.5 %; Calcium: 14.9 %; Magnesium: 9.4%.

Swedish Meatballs And Gravy

Swedish meatballs made with a blend of seasoned ground beef and turkey baked in the oven and tossed with a creamy dairy free sauce. Delicious and easy recipe that saves time and reduces dirty dishes.

Course: Main   Serves 4   Ready in 45 minutes   GF, DF, P, W30

INGREDIENTS

Meatballs:
1 pound ground beef
1 pound ground turkey (you can also use pork or chicken)
1 large onion, minced
3 garlic cloves, minced
1 large egg
2 slices gluten free bread turned into bread crumbs (omit if paleo or whole30)
3 tbsp plant milk
1 ½ tsp Celtic sea salt
1 tsp dried rosemary
1/2 tsp black pepper
1 tsp smoked paprika
1 tsp coriander
3 tbsp avocado oil, for sautéing

Dairy free sauce:
4 tbsp plant based butter
4-5 tbsp cassava flour or 3 tbsp arrowroot powder
3 cups beef or chicken stock
1 tbsp brown mustard (stone ground)
1 cup coconut cream
1 tsp onion powder
1 tsp garlic powder

DIRECTIONS

1. Make the meatballs. Heat avocado oil in a large skillet over medium heat and sauté the onions and garlic until soft. Set aside to cool down because we're going to add all the other ingredients in the same skillet to save dirty dishes.

Toast and ground the gluten free bread (store bought or homemade) into bread crumbs with a food processor. Don't use breadcrumbs if you want a paleo or whole30 version.

To the sautéed onions and garlic, add the bread crumbs, the egg, plant milk, seasonings, the ground beef and the ground turkey. With your hand, mix well to combine, then roll into evenly sized meatballs. Place on 1 or 2 deep (9x13") baking dishes (single layer). Bake in a preheated oven at 425 F for 25-30 minutes. So they could get a nice brown color on the surface.

2. Prepare the sauce. In a skillet melt the plant based butter over medium-heat. Add cassava flour, cook and whisk until golden brown and bubbly, about 3 minutes.

Then slowly pour in the beef stock. While whisking add the rest of ingredients. Mix until everything is incorporated. Turn off the heat.

3. Remove the meatballs from the oven and pour the dairy free sauce in the same baking dish where the meatballs were baked. The juices leaked from the meatballs will add extra flavor to the gravy. Return to the oven for another 5-10 minutes to warm them up. Then serve over mashed veggies (I used half potatoes and half cauliflower).

Serving size: 1/4 of portion: Calories: 781.8; Total Fat: 51.2; Sugar: 14 g; Total carbohydrate: 31.5 g; Protein: 51.2 g; Vitamin A: 7.3 %; Vitamin B-6: 22.2 %; Vitamin B-12: 46.2 %; Vitamin C: 7.9 %; Iron: 25 %; Calcium: 4 %; Magnesium: 10.6 %; Zinc: 31.6 %.

Bean Stuffed Bell Peppers

Simple, healthy, flavorful, and filling vegan stuffed peppers that can be enjoyed by nearly everyone. An easy meal prep friendly lunch, dinner or freezer meal.

Course: Main   Serves 3 people   Ready in 1 h 15 minutes   GF, DF, V

INGREDIENTS

6 medium bell peppers

Stuffing:

2 cups navy beans, cooked
1 cup cauliflower florets, diced
1 large onion, diced
4 fresh garlic cloves, minced
1 large carrot, diced
1/2 cup marinara sauce (or diced tomatoes with minimum liquid)
1 ½ tsp Celtic sea salt
1/2 tsp black pepper
1 ½ tsp dried thyme
1 ½ tsp paprika (use smoked paprika for more flavor)
1/2 tsp cumin
3 tbsp oil, for sautéing

DIRECTIONS

1. Preheat oven to 360 F.

2. In a skillet over medium heat, sauté onions and garlic until soft, about 3 minutes. Add in carrots, cauliflower and cook for 5 additional minutes.

3. Stir in the beans (no liquid), the marinara sauce and all the seasonings. Cook for 3 more minutes. Remove from heat.

4. While the mixture is cooling a bit, prepare the peppers. Remove tops (stem) from peppers and scrape out the insides. Steam for 1-2 minutes (for faster baking).

5. Fill the peppers with bean mixture pushing it down so they are tightly filled. Place in a baking dish, cover with a lid.

6. Bake in preheated oven for 45 min to 1 hour or until peppers have softened. There will be some liquid accumulated at the bottom. If you want you can keep it for a future soup or discard it.

Notes And Suggestions

Dried white beans or canned can be used. To make this dish paleo and whole30 friendly, remove the beans and use more cauliflower or other veggies.

To freeze: store in an airtight container. To reheat: thaw in the fridge the night before. Then in a 350F preheated oven heat them for 20 minutes until they are heated throughout.

Serving size: 2 stuffed peppers: Calories: 346; Total Fat: 10.5; Sugar: 6.5 g; Total carbohydrate: 55 g; Protein: 12.4 g; Vitamin A: 438.3 %; Vitamin B-6: 23 %; Vitamin C: 815.5 %; Iron: 31.8 %; Calcium: 13.9 %; Magnesium: 21.4%; Zinc: 9.5 %.

Spaghetti Squash & Honey Mustard Chicken

Super flavorful roasted chicken breasts marinated in a honey mustard sauce served with spaghetti squash "noodles". This is a healthier pasta alternative for those who want to avoid it.

Course: Main   Serves 2   Ready in 45-55 minutes   GF, DF, P

INGREDIENTS

2 medium chicken breasts
1 medium spaghetti squash
5-6 kale leaves, chopped
salt and pepper to season the squash
2 tsp of avocado oil, to brush the squash

Sauce:

1/3 cup honey mustard sauce (see page 230)
2 garlic cloves, minced
1/4 onion, minced (or powder)
1 tsp dried thyme
1 tsp basil leaves, dried
3/4 tsp sea salt
1/4 tsp black pepper

DIRECTIONS

1. To prepare the spaghetti squash preheat oven to 425 F and cut the squash in half across the length, remove the seeds. Drizzle some oil, sprinkle salt and pepper on top and bake in the oven for 40-50 minutes - upside down. When cooled, separate the strands into long "noodles" with a fork.

2. Make the sauce. Combine all the ingredients in a bowl. Reserve 1/4 of the sauce for later. Place the chicken breasts (cut into smaller strips) in the bowl and mix to coat. Let sit at the room temperature for 15 minutes before cooking.

3. Roast the chicken. Place the chicken breasts in a roasting pan in a single layer. Roast (uncovered) at 400 F until they get a little golden brown but still soft inside, about 20-25 minutes depending on the size of the pieces. Add the chopped kale (mixed with the reserved sauce) for the last 5 minutes before you take the chicken out of the oven.

4. To serve scrape the squash meat off (with a fork) directly onto serving plates. Top with chicken and spoon the pan juices over. Serve while warm.

Notes And Suggestions

If you have large chicken breasts, you can slice them in smaller pieces, the sauce will cover more surfaces.

You can also bake the spaghetti squash and marinate the chicken the day before and get the meal ready in 30 minutes

Serving size: 1 breast + 1.5 cup squash noodles: Calories: 634; Total Fat: 33.8 g; Fiber: 8.1 %; Carbohydrate: 47.3 g; Sugars: 24.7 g; Protein: 39.7 g; Vitamin A: 541.9 %; Vitamin B-12: 15 %; Vitamin C: 152.5 %; Iron: 26.5 %; Calcium: 22.8 %.

| Main Dishes

Baked Cod With Basil Pesto Sauce

This perfect, flaky, oven baked cod is one of the easiest fish dishes you can make. And the lemony basil pesto sauce kicks it up to the next level with a lovely fresh aroma.

Course: Main   Serves 2   Ready in 25 minutes   GF, DF, P, W30

INGREDIENTS

Baked cod fillets:

2 (6-ounce) pieces cod, boneless and skinless
sea salt, to taste
freshly ground black pepper, to taste
4 tbsp creamy basil pesto sauce (see page 234)
1 tsp chopped chives, to garnish

Zucchini noodles:

1 large zucchini
1 tbsp olive oil
2 garlic cloves, finely minced
salt and pepper to taste

DIRECTIONS

1. Preheat oven to 400 F.

2. Pat dry the cod pieces and place in a baking dish. Season fish with a little sea salt and freshly ground black pepper.

3. Bake for 15-20 minutes or until fish flakes easily with a fork.

4. Remove from oven and place each piece on a separate serving plate. Drizzle 2 tablespoons of the basil sauce over top of fish and serve along your favorite salad.

5. To make the zucchini noodles, use a julienne peeler to make long thin noodles. Heat 1 tablespoon of olive oil in a sauté pan over medium high heat. Once the oil is hot, add the minced garlic and sauté for 30 seconds.

6. Add the zucchini noodles and sauté until they just start to get tender (about 3 minutes). Season with salt and pepper as needed and remove from heat directly to serving plates.

Notes And Suggestions

You can also use any kind of mild white fish like halibut, sea bass, pollock, haddock, these will all work great. Serve it alongside a green salad, steamed vegetables (like zucchini noodles) or some cauliflower rice.

Serving size: 6 oz fillet & pesto: Calories: 202.2; Total Fat: 2.9 g; Fiber: 8.1 %; Carbohydrate: 2 g; Sugars: 0.7 g; Protein: 38.7 g; Vitamin A: 7.2 %; Vitamin B-6: 25.4 %; Vitamin B-12: 29.8 %; Vitamin C: 6.1 %; Iron: 26.5 %; Calcium: 3.7 %; Magnesium: 20.7 %.

Juicy Sirloin Steak With Mixed Green Salad

Marinated top sirloin steak seared and baked in the oven to perfection. For maximum flavor it is topped with a quick pan sauce and served with a mixed green salad dressed with homemade balsamic vinaigrette.

Course: Main   **Serves 1**   **Ready in 40 minutes**   GF, DF, P, W30

INGREDIENTS

¾ inch-thick top sirloin steak
2 tbsp avocado oil, for searing

Marinade:

4 tbsp avocado oil
4 tbsp balsamic vinegar
1 tbsp stone ground mustard
dash of sea salt
dash of black pepper
1 tsp minced garlic
1 tsp minced onion or powder
1 tsp dried rosemary

Salad:

1 cup mixed greens
1/2 cup arugula microgreens
3 cherry tomatoes
1/2 bell pepper
1 tbsp pumpkin seeds
1 tbsp cranberries (dried)
drizzle with balsamic vinaigrette dressing (for recipe see page 222)

DIRECTIONS

1. Mix all ingredients for the marinade; reserve 2 tbsp of the marinade for later. Add steak to marinade, cover and refrigerate overnight, turning occasionally. Remove from the marinade, pat dry and season lightly with salt and pepper.

2. In a large skillet or griddle pan (oven proof) heat avocado oil over moderately high heat until it's sizzling hot and add the steak. Cook 1.5 minutes on each side and transfer to a preheated oven (375 F) for 3-4 min (for medium-rare meat - internal temperature - 145 F) and 6-7 min (for medium). Remove from the oven and transfer to a small platter.

3. To the released meat juice (in the skillet) add the reserved marinade and bring to a simmer, stirring for 2-3 minutes. Spoon glaze over steak when ready to serve.

4. Gather and mix the salad ingredients. Drizzle with balsamic vinaigrette dressing right before serving.

Notes And Suggestions

Because this type of meat is very lean, it can be dry and chewy, it should always be tenderized with marinade and do not overcook.

Remove steak from refrigerator 30 min before cooking to bring to room temperature

Depending on how thick the stake is and how hot your stove gets, the timing will need to be monitored and adjusted.

Serving size: 6 oz marinated steak: Calories: 579.2; Total Fat: 38.9 g; Total carbohydrate: 6.7 g; Dietary Fiber: 0.8 g; Sugars: 1 g; Protein: 52 g; Vitamin A: 0.8 %; Vitamin B-12: 80.8%; Vitamin B-6: 41.7 %; Vitamin C: 3.9 %; Iron: 34.2 %; Calcium: 4.2 %.

Caramelized Asian Salmon Bowl

Pan seared salmon fillet smothered in a luscious sauce and then seared to create a charred exterior. To make a complete meal serve with roasted vegetables and a fresh green salad.

Course: Main   Serves 2 people   Ready in 1 hour   GF, DF, P, W30

INGREDIENTS

Salmon:

2 (6-8 oz. each) salmon fillets
sesame seeds, sprinkle, optional

For the glaze:

4 tbsp coconut aminos
(alternative to soy sauce)
2 tbsp olive oil, extra virgin
1 tbsp tomato paste, or whole30
approved ketchup
1 tsp onion powder, or 1 tbsp
minced fresh onion
1 tsp garlic powder
1 tsp finely minced garlic
1 tsp smoked paprika
3/4 tsp sea salt
1/4 tsp black pepper

Roasted vegetables:

1 medium sweet potato, cut into
strips
1/2 medium onion, sliced
1 red bell pepper, sliced

For the salad:

1 cup of mixed greens
1/4 cup sliced cucumbers
1/4 cup sliced raw carrots
1 tbsp creamy avocado dressing
(see page 228)

DIRECTIONS

1. Roast the vegetables. In order to have the vegetables roasted in time to serve with salmon, place them in the oven first. Cut the sweet potatoes, the bell pepper and the onion into strips.

2. Prepare the sauce (glaze): mix all ingredients in a small container. Take 2 tbsp of the glaze and drizzle over veggies to cover them evenly. Place in the preheated oven (400 F) in a single layer and roast for 40-50 minutes.

3. Cook the salmon. Meanwhile remove the salmon from the refrigerator about 15 to 20 minutes before you are ready to start cooking. Pat salmon dry with paper towels and brush with the glaze. Let it absorb the acidity for 10 minutes.

4. In a skillet, drizzle some olive oil around the pan and then place the fillets, skin side up, in the skillet. Cook salmon over medium-high heat 2-3 minutes in order to create a charred exterior.

5. Use a spatula and flip the salmon. Brush with another layer of sauce and transfer the skillet in the preheated oven and bake for another 10-12 minutes.

6. Assemble the bowl. Prepare the greens and the fresh chopped vegetables. Place everything along with the roasted vegetables and the salmon in a bowl and drizzle a bit of avocado dressing and sesame seeds over the salad.

Notes And Suggestions

If you prefer to avoid frying, cook the salmon (glazed) in the oven from the start. But charring is not guaranteed unless you use the broil function for the last minutes of cooking.

Serving size: 6 oz salmon & vegetable bowl: Calories: 575.9; Total Fat: 28.9 g; Total carbohydrate: 49.1 g; Dietary Fiber: 9.5 g; Sugars: 14.3 g; Protein: 38.4 g; Vitamin A: 566.1 %; Vitamin B-12: 86.4%; Vitamin B-6: 114.1 %; Vitamin C: 166.8; Iron: 19.5 %.

Sweet Butternut Squash Casserole

The sweet and creamy chunks of butternut squash and sweet potatoes together with the nutty rice and sweet tang of cranberries bring a flavorful earthly sweetness in a single dish. This is great as a side dish on a holiday table or served by itself.

Course: Main   Serves 6-7 people   Ready in 1 hour   GF, DF, V

INGREDIENTS

1 medium butternut squash, cubed
1 large sweet potato, cubed
3/4 cup dried cranberries
1/2 cup golden raisins
1/2 cup short grain brown rice
1/4 cup wild rice
1/6 tsp nutmeg
1 tsp cinnamon
3/4 tsp Celtic sea salt
1/4 black pepper
3 tbsp maple syrup
4 tbsp extra virgin olive oil or avocado oil
1 ½ tbsp apple cider vinegar or balsamic vinegar

DIRECTIONS

1. Preheat oven to 400 F. Prepare a parchment paper lined baking sheet, the larger the better.

2. In a small bowl combine the oil, maple syrup, vinegar and the rest of the seasonings. Stir to combine.

3. In a large bowl, combine cubed butternut squash (peeled and seeded), cubed sweet potatoes, and add half of the seasoned liquid mixture we made earlier, toss to mix.

4. Place the cubed veggies in a single layer on the baking sheet (use 2 baking sheets if necessary) to get an even roast on all sides. Bake for 35 minutes, turning once half-way through baking, until softened and with a golden brown crust.

5. Meanwhile cook the rice. Place the rinsed rice in a pot with boiling water (use a 2 to 1 water to rice ratio). Add the other half of seasoned liquid mixture, stir, cover the pot with the lid, and reduce the heat to its very lowest setting to help the rice cook evenly (for about 20 minutes). Remove from heat, add the cranberries and the raisins. Cover again and let it sit, so the steam will plump the rice and fruits.

6. The veggies and rice will likely be ready at the same time. To arrange the meal and serve, take a taller baking dish (I used a 9x13" glass dish) and place a layer of veggies, then a layer of rice and repeat until you fill up the dish. Serve warm or reheat for later.

Notes And Suggestions

The best way to get a perfectly cooked rice is to soak for at least 2 hours or overnight before cooking.

Feel free to add other veggies (like beets, carrots, parsnips) or nuts to the dish.

Serving size: 1 ½ cup: Calories: 304.7; Total Fat: 8.2 g; Total carbohydrate: 61.4 g; Dietary Fiber: 7.4 g; Sugars: 28 g; Protein: 3.1 g; Vitamin A: 326.3 %; Vitamin B-6: 16.1 %; Vitamin C: 59.7; Calcium: 9.4; Iron: 10.5 %; Magnesium: 16.1.

Baked Chicken Thighs With Asparagus

Bathed in a garlicky lemon mustard sauce and bursting with Mediterranean flavors, these crispy-skinned baked chicken thighs with asparagus make an easy delicious sheet pan dinner with minimal clean up.

Course: Main   Serves 2   Ready in 1 hour   GF, DF, P, W30

INGREDIENTS

4 chicken thighs
1 pound asparagus, ends trimmed
a mix of spring greens, for serving

Marinade:

2 tbsp olive oil, extra virgin
1 tbsp Dijon mustard
1 tbsp stone ground brown mustard
2 tbsp lemon juice
2 tbsp maple syrup
1 tbsp oregano, dried
1/2 tsp thyme
1 tsp onion powder
4 garlic cloves, finely minced
3/4 tsp sea salt
1/4 tsp black pepper

DIRECTIONS

1. Preheat your oven to 425 F. In a small bowl prepare the marinade by mixing everything together.

2. Place the chicken thighs in the marinade coating well each of them and let sit at room temperature for 15-20 minutes to absorb the flavors and tenderize.

3. Meanwhile rinse and dry asparagus. Remove the woody ends (about 1 inch). Set aside. When ready, place chicken thighs skin-side up on a rimmed baking sheet. Do not wipe off the marinade.

4. Bake for 30 minutes then add the asparagus (coating well the spears in the sheet juices) for the last 10 minutes of roasting time. If you like them softer, add them in during the last 15 minutes.

5. Remove from oven, let rest 5 minutes. Then serve over a bed of greens, or other salad. Choose your favorite salad dressing for you greens.

Notes And Suggestions

Choose bone-in skin-on chicken thighs as the meat is so much more flavorful and the skin gets nice and crispy. Plus they are much easier to cook without drying out.

Serving size 2 thighs and 1/2 lb asparagus: Calories: 559; Total Fat: 34.2 g; Total carbohydrate: 26.6 g; Fiber: 0.9 g; Sugars: 12.8 g; Protein: 40.6 g; Vitamin A: 54.1 %; Vitamin B-6: 3.6 %; Vitamin C: 51 %; Calcium: 15.8%; Iron: 23.2 %; Magnesium: 13.3 %.

| Main Dishes

Easy One Pan Cabbage Skillet

Tender cabbage and tangy tomatoes that pair perfectly with the ground beef and rice - ready in less than an hour. An easy quick meal perfect on a weeknight with minimal clean up.

Course: Main   Serves 5   Ready in 40 minutes   GF, DF

INGREDIENTS

1/2 medium cabbage, chopped
1 cup Basmati rice (cooked)
8 oz organic bacon or 1/2 lb lean ground beef
1 large onion, diced
2 garlic cloves, minced
2 cups diced tomatoes
2 tbsp tomato paste
1 large bell pepper, chopped
3/4 tsp powdered rosemary
3/4 tsp sea salt
1/2 tsp ground black pepper
6-7 kale leaves, chopped
2 tbsp olive oil or avocado oil

DIRECTIONS

1. Paraboil (precook) the rice in advance or use some cooked rice (leftovers). Rinse 1/2 cup of rice and place in a saucepan with 1.5 cups of boiling water. Add a pinch of salt and boil for 5 minutes. Drain and cool.

2. Heat the oil in a large skillet over medium high heat. Add the onion and cook for 2-3 minutes or until softened. Stir in the garlic, cooking for 1 minute longer. Then add bacon, or the ground beef and cook until browned, approximately 3-4 minutes.

3. Add the tomatoes, bell pepper and tomato paste to the skillet. Season with salt, pepper and rosemary. Cook for about 3-4 minutes.

4. Meanwhile chop the cabbage and add to the skillet, give it a good stir and cook (reduce heat to low) for 10-15 minutes covered with a lid.

5. At the end add the chopped kale, give it a stir. Remove from heat, allow to rest for 10-15 minutes and serve!

Notes And Suggestions

If by the end the mixture start to stick to the bottom, add 1/3 cup of water.

For a more pronounced and sweeter taste add 3-4 tbsp of Coconut Aminos seasoning.

Serving size 1.3 cup: Calories: 207.9; Total Fat: 7.2 g; Total carbohydrate: 24.6 g; Fiber: 4.6 g; Sugars: 9.1 g; Protein: 12 g; Vitamin A: 20 %; Vitamin B-6: 6.8 %; Vitamin C: 138.6 %; Calcium: 14.8%; Iron: 11.6 %; Magnesium: 2.6 %.

Soups

The soups are quick and easy to make because everything can be thrown into one pot plus they are full of nutrients and flavor when you use fresh vegetables. These clean-eating soup recipes are all made with real, whole foods without using cans, boxes or bullion cubes. Whenever a recipe calls for stock or broth try to use a homemade version, it makes a huge difference in taste.

Shiitake Mushroom Vegetable Soup

Super flavorful vegetable soup with shiitake mushrooms that has a rich "creamy" taste without using any dairy / non dairy ingredients or thickening agents. The meaty flesh of the shiitake mushroom cap has a full-bodied flavor that pairs perfectly with any type of meat, or you can make it vegan if you like.

Course: Soup   **Serves 4 people**   **Ready in 45 minutes**   GF, DF

INGREDIENTS

20 medium shiitake mushrooms, fresh, chopped
3-4 slices sugar free bacon (turkey, or pork)
1 large onion, diced
1/2 stalk of leek, chopped
5 garlic cloves, minced
2 medium potatoes, cubed
2 medium carrots, cubed
1 cup crushed tomatoes
1 can of cooked chickpeas
1 tsp coriander
1/2 tsp smoked paprika
1/2 tsp mustard powder
2 bay leaves
1 tsp rosemary
1 tsp pink salt
1/3 tsp cracked black pepper
4 cups of water (or stock)

DIRECTIONS

1. Add the bacon to a wide, large pot and cook it, until it gets crispy and has released a lot of fat. Reserve the bacon and set aside.

2. To the bacon fat, add the diced onions, leeks, garlic and some oil, if needed. Season with salt, pepper and the rest of the herbs and spices, cook until they are soft and aromatic, about 5 minutes. Add the chopped mushrooms to the pan, and cook until they are soft, about 6 to 7 minutes. Scoop 1/3 of the mushroom mixture into a bowl, reserve for serving.

3. To the same pot, add the diced potatoes, carrots, drained chickpeas, and the crushed tomatoes. Add the water and bring to a boil. Reduce to a simmer and cook for 25-30 min. Taste and season with more salt, if needed.

4. You can serve the soup as it is or puree it. Using a blender or immersion blender, puree the soup until smooth. Return the soup to the pot and add the reserved bacon (thinly chopped) and mushrooms. Taste the soup and adjust the seasoning, if needed. Garnish with the chopped fresh herbs if you like.

Notes And Suggestions

If you want the soup to be silkier, you can add some coconut cream or cashew cream.

Store the soup in an air-tight container in the refrigerator for up to 4 days, or you can freeze it for up to a month.

Serving size: 2 cups: Calories: 297.3; Total Fat: 2.9 g; Total carbohydrate: 60.1 g; Dietary Fiber: 10.4 g; Sugars: 8 g; Protein: 13.9 g; Vitamin A: 107.4 %; Vitamin C: 42.4 %; Iron: 19.2 %; Calcium: 9.3%.

Meatless Beet Soup (Borscht)

A healthier version of the traditional Eastern European soup (borscht) made with beets, red sauerkraut and other root vegetables. All these bring sweet-and-sour hues and a beautiful bright red color - completely vegan, perfect for a meatless Monday meal or for a gentle detox.

Course: Soup   Serves 4-5 people   Ready in 1 hour   GF, DF, V, W30

INGREDIENTS

3 medium beet roots, peeled, cubed
1 large red onion, diced
1 large carrot, diced
4 garlic cloves, minced
3 medium potatoes, cubed
1 cup white beans, pre-cooked (omit if whole30 and paleo)
1 cup red cabbage sauerkraut (homemade, or use white sauerkraut)
2 tbsp olive oil, for searing
1/2 tsp Celtic sea salt
1/3 tsp black pepper
2 bay leaves
1/3 tsp coriander
7 cups filtered water
1/3 cup chopped parsley (or dill) to serve

DIRECTIONS

1. Add the olive oil into a large pot. Over medium heat, sauté the onion and garlic for about 3 to 5 minutes, stirring once or twice. Add the spices.

2. Add the potatoes, carrots and beets. Stir again. Continue sautéeing for another few minutes.

3. Add the sauerkraut, beans and the water. Stir to combine. Simmer the soup, covered, over low to medium heat for 30-40 minutes or until the beets are tender. Your cook time may vary depending on how small you chopped them. (If it's your first time cooking the soup, you may want to check on it a few times.

4. Taste and season with salt (if you need). Ladle into a bowl and serve with chopped greens if desired.

Notes And Suggestions

This beet soup will keep in the fridge in an airtight container for up to 1 week. It freezes beautifully too: simply cool the soup and place it into a freezer-safe container, leaving an inch of space at the top for expansion. Freeze for up to 2 months.

If you don't have sauerkraut, use the juice of a lemon plus 1 cup of diced tomatoes (these will replace the sourness in the sauerkraut). If using this method make sure to increase the amount of salt according to your taste.

Serving size: 2 cups: Calories: 260.3; Total Fat: 6.1 g; Total carbohydrate: 45.9 g; Dietary Fiber: 9 g; Sugars: 10.3 g; Protein: 8.3 g; Vitamin A: 58.5%; Vitamin B-6: 29.2%; Vitamin C: 68.9 %; Iron: 21.6 %; Calcium: 9.6%

| Soups

Creamy Cauliflower Soup

This velvety-smooth cauliflower soup has complex flavors and is made with basic ingredients. It's filling, rich and easy to make, naturally vegan and gluten free. Serve it with a few slices of your favorite gluten free crusty bread for a light dinner or lunch.

Course: Soup   Makes 8 cups   Ready in 50 minutes   GF, DF, V, W30

INGREDIENTS

1 medium head of cauliflower, cut into florets
1 large yellow onion, chopped
1 parsnip, sliced
1 large carrot, chopped
2 tbsp olive oil, extra virgin
5 cloves of garlic, chopped
2 large potatoes (or 3/4 cup white beans)
2 cups of water
3 cups of stock (vegetable or chicken)
3 tbsp coconut cream
1 tsp Celtic sea salt
1/4 tsp black pepper
2 bay leaves
1/3 tsp cumin powder
1/3 tsp rosemary, dried
1.5 tbsp lemon juice
chopped greens for garnish
coconut aminos (optional finish)

DIRECTIONS

1. In a soup pot add the water and the stock. When it's about to boil, turn the heat down a bit and add the chopped potatoes, carrots, parsnip (celery root is an excellent alternative to parsnip) and the bay leaves. Let it slowly simmer.

2. Meanwhile heat a skillet with olive oil. Add the onion, cook, stirring occasionally, until it turns translucent, then add the garlic and half of the cauliflower to give it a little roast (keep a few roasted florets for garnish if you want). At this time you can add all the seasonings. The remaining cauliflower transfer to the simmering pot.

3. Once the cauliflower from the skillet starts to soften and turn slightly brown on edges, transfer all the content to the simmering pot as well. Cook (gently simmering) for 20-25 minutes, stirring occasionally, so the flavors have time to meld. Add the lemon juice.

4. Once the vegetables look soft in cooked through, remove the pot from the heat and let it cool a bit. Remove the bay leaves, then, transfer the soup to a blender, make sure yours is heat proof (I did it in two batches to avoid overflowing).

5. Add the coconut cream and blend until smooth. Taste and add additional salt or sourness if necessary. Top individual bowls of soup, sprinkle with chopped greens and microgreens. Garnish with a drizzle of coconut aminos. Serve hot.

Keep the soup in the refrigerator, covered, for up to 4-5 days.

Serving size: 2 cups: Calories: 223.8; Total Fat: 7.7 g; Total carbohydrate: 34.9 g; Dietary Fiber: 8.1 g; Sugars: 7.4 g; Protein: 8.3 g; Vitamin A: 144.3%; Vitamin B-6: 25.4 %; Vitamin C: 179.4 %; Iron: 13.2%; Calcium: 10.3 %; Magnesium: 16%.

Moldovan Chicken Soup

Healthy, tangy and light, bursting with chicken flavor packed with veggies and fresh bone broth, no noodles here. This is an Eastern European (Moldovan) inspired chicken soup made from scratch with fresh ingredients - the perfect remedy for anyone who feels under the weather.

Course: Soup   Serves 7-8 people   Ready in 1 h 20 min   GF, DF, W30

INGREDIENTS

2 lb chicken wings or a small chicken (organic)
12 cups filtered water
1 medium onion diced
1 large carrot, peeled and diced
2 small celery stalks, chopped
1/2 cup celery root, peeled, diced
4 potatoes, peeled, cubed
1 red bell pepper, diced
1 large tomato, diced
3 cloves of garlic, minced
1 tsp thyme or 2 sprigs - fresh
1/2 tsp dried dill weed
2 bay leaves
1/2 tsp black pepper
5 tbsp lemon juice or sauerkraut juice
1 ½ tbsp Celtic sea salt
2 tablespoons fresh parsley, minced (to garnish)

DIRECTIONS

1. Wash the chicken, place it in a deep saucepan and add filtered water (about 12 cups).

2. Bring to a boil, spoon off any foam or scum that rises to the top. To the pot add 2 bay leaves, the black pepper and the dried herbs. Reduce the heat and simmer on low heat (about 15 minutes) until you prepare the rest of the veggies.

3. Clean and finely chop the carrot, potatoes, onion, garlic, celery root and stalks. Add those to the pot and the salt. Simmer for 20 minutes.

4. Then add the diced tomato, bell pepper and lemon juice. Simmer for another 15-20 minutes and turn off the heat.

5. At this time you can add to the pot the fresh chopped herbs, or you can save them and sprinkle some on top of the soup bowls, as you serve.

6. Taste and adjust the seasoning if it's needed.

Let the soup sit for 15-20 minutes or more before serving, it will allow the flavors to blend in better.

Notes And Suggestions

When choosing the type of chicken parts to use in soup, opt for more bones and connective tissue because the marrow in the bones adds much more flavor plus collagen: like whole chicken, chicken feet, thighs, the frame of a roasted chicken, chicken backs and wings.

Add some cooked rice or grains in the soup for a boost of flavor and protein (if not paleo or whole30).

Serving size: 2 cups: Calories: 201.7; Total Fat: 6.8 g; Total carbohydrate: 23.6 g; Dietary Fiber: 4.5 g; Sugars: 3.2 g; Protein: 11.9 g; Vitamin A: 53.7 %; Vitamin B-6: 28.1 %; Vitamin B-12: 2%; Vitamin C: 71.7 %; Iron: 8.2 %; Calcium: 4.7 %; Selenium: 12% .

Rustic Mushroom Potato Soup

This easy soup is loaded with whole food vegan ingredients like white button mushrooms, potatoes, aromatic herbs and spices. The addition of coconut cream adds a touch of creamy richness, but the soup is still delicious without it.

Course: Soup   Serves 4 people   Ready in 40 min   GF, DF, V, W30

INGREDIENTS

16 oz white button mushrooms, sliced
5 cups of filtered water
4 medium potatoes, cubed
2 tbsp extra virgin olive oil
1 large yellow onion, chopped
2 carrots, grated, or diced
3 cloves of garlic, minced
2 tbsp fresh lemon juice
4-5 tbsp coconut cream (from a can)
1/2 tsp black pepper
2 bay leaves
1 tsp sea salt
1 ½ tsp rosemary, dried or 2 fresh sprigs
fresh chopped parsley, to garnish

DIRECTIONS

1. In a medium pot combine water the cubed potatoes and the bay leaves and simmer on low heat until the potatoes start to get soft.

2. Meanwhile, in a large skillet (heated), sauté the onions with olive oil until golden. Then add the sliced mushrooms and continue cooking until the liquid starts to form. Then add the grated carrots, garlic, rosemary, salt and pepper. Cook for 2 minutes stirring occasionally.

3. Pour the mushroom mixture over the boiling potatoes in the pot. Add the lemon juice, and the coconut cream and cook for another 2-3 minutes and turn off the heat. Taste and add more salt if necessary.

4. Allow the flavors to meld for at least 15 minutes before serving. Ladle into bowls and garnish with fresh chopped parsley or chopped kale.

Notes And Suggestions

Serve warm. Or transfer to sealed container(s) and refrigerate for up to 4 days.

Serving size: 2 cups; Calories: 227.1; Total Fat: 7.2 g; Total carbohydrate: 33.8 g; Dietary Fiber: 4.4 g; Sugars: 5.8 g; Protein: 8.2 g; Vitamin A: 84.4 %; Vitamin B-6: 3.8 %; Vitamin C: 51.3 %; Iron: 10.8 %; Calcium: 4.1 %; Selenium: 13.2 %.

Chunky Leek Soup

An easy and lighter leek soup that unlike it's creamy classic version, which uses milk and cream, it's left to have a chunky texture. The flavors are build with the help of stock and a variety of vegetables - cooked until tender. This can be blended as well if desired.

Course: Soup   Serves 5   Ready in 40 minutes   GF, DF, V, W30

INGREDIENTS

3 leeks, trimmed, chopped
1 medium onion, diced
2 large carrots, diced
1 small bell pepper, diced
1 tbsp tomato paste
1 small parsnip, diced
1/4 small celery root, diced
2 medium potatoes, cubed
1 tsp paprika
2/3 tsp Celtic sea salt
3 tbsp avocado oil (for sautéing)
4-5 cups of vegetable stock (or use chicken stock if not vegan)
dash of black pepper

DIRECTIONS

1. Wash and prepare all vegetables, dice (as fine as possible) and cube them.

2. Meanwhile, in a large skillet (heated), sauté the leeks and onions with oil until golden. Then add the rest of the vegetables, sauté for another 3-4 minutes. Add the stock, the tomato paste and the seasonings.

3. Continue cooking until everything gets soft and tender (about 15 - 20 minutes). Taste and add more salt if necessary.

4. Turn off the heat and allow the flavors to meld for at least 15 minutes before serving. Ladle into bowls and garnish with fresh chopped parsley or other greens.

Notes And Suggestions

Serve warm. Or transfer to sealed container(s) and refrigerate for up to 4 days

To make the soup creamy, use a blender and add a few tablespoons of coconut cream.

To replace the tomato paste use a tbsp of lemon juice.

Serving size: 2 cups; Calories: 186.7; Total Fat: 6.4 g; Total carbohydrate: 30.1 g; Dietary Fiber: 5 g; Sugars: 7.5 g; Protein: 3.2 g; Vitamin A: 88.4 %; Vitamin B-6: 12.8 %; Vitamin C: 59.3 %; Iron: 12.8 %; Calcium: 9.2 %; Magnesium: 7.3 %.

Cream Of Asparagus Soup

A flavorful creamy asparagus soup made in just one pot, that is done in 30 minutes from start to finish. Enjoy it as an appetizer with a spoon or from a mug, or add some protein if you prefer a more substantial meal.

Course: Soup   Serves 4   Ready in 30 minutes   GF, DF, V, W30

INGREDIENTS

1 ½ lb asparagus (about 22 spears) ends trimmed
1/2 small celery root (celeriac), diced
2 tbsp avocado oil (for sautéing)
1 leek, chopped
4 garlic cloves, chopped
3-4 cups of vegetable stock (or use chicken stock if not vegan)
1 large potato, chopped (optional, for creaminess)
1/2 cup coconut cream
1 ½ tsp lemon juice
1/2 tsp coriander powder
1 tsp rosemary, dried or fresh
dash of black pepper
salt to taste
1 tbsp parsley, chopped, to garnish

DIRECTIONS

1. Heat the oil in a large pot over medium-high heat. Add in the chopped leek, garlic, coriander, rosemary and pepper and sauté for 2-3 minutes until the leek starts to soften.

2. Add in the diced celery root and sauté another 2-3 minutes, then add the asparagus, potato (finely chopped) the stock and bring to a boil. When the soup is boiling, cover with a lid, lower the heat to medium-low and simmer for 10-15 minutes or until the asparagus is tender.

3. Remove from heat and mix in the coconut cream and lemon juice. Use an immersion stick or better - a blender to purèe the soup until it is smooth.

4. Taste and season with more salt and pepper. Ladle into bowls and serve the soup topped with chopped parsley or other fresh greens.

Notes And Suggestions

I used potato as a thickener and to give the soup body. If you would prefer to avoid nightshades/potatoes, substitute it with 1 cup of chopped cauliflower.

The soup can be made one day ahead. Once prepared, let cool; cover and refrigerate for up to 3 days. Rewarm before serving.

Serving size: 1 ½ cups; Calories: 226; Total Fat: 12.9 g; Total carbohydrate: 25.2 g; Dietary Fiber: 5.9 g; Sugars: 5.4 g; Protein: 4.8 g; Vitamin A: 12.4 %; Vitamin B-6: 19.2 %; Vitamin C: 45.6 %; Iron: 11.5 %; Calcium: 5.6 %; Magnesium: 10.1 %; Zinc: 4.7 %.

Cream Of Mushroom Soup

This soup is one of the easiest you can make and it's ready in under 30 minutes. It's silky, smooth, velvety texture makes a flavorful base to dishes like casseroles, soups, or rich sauces for chicken and beef. Or enjoy it by itself with a toasted slice of gluten free bread.

Course: Soup   Makes 6 cups   Ready in 30 minutes   GF, DF, V, P, W30

INGREDIENTS

8 oz white button mushrooms, sliced
8 oz whole baby portobello mushrooms, sliced
4 oz whole oyster mushrooms, sliced
3 tbsp avocado oil (for sautéing) or use vegan butter
2 medium onions, chopped
4 garlic cloves, minced
2 ½ cups of vegetable stock (or use chicken stock if not vegan)
1/2 cup coconut cream, or cashew cream
2 ½ tbsp arrowroot powder
2 tbsp apple cider vinegar
1 tbsp Dijon mustard
1 tbsp fresh thyme leaves
1 tbsp fresh rosemary leaves, chopped
dash of black pepper
salt to taste (about 1/4 tsp)
1 tbsp parsley, chopped, to garnish

DIRECTIONS

1. Heat a large skillet over medium-high heat with oil. Add the onion, thyme, rosemary, pepper and cook until golden.

2. Then add the mushrooms, cook for about 5 minutes, until tender and they released the juices.

3. At this stage you can add the apple cider vinegar, garlic and the arrowroot powder, stir until everything is incorporated and let it cook for 1-2 minutes. Then add the stock and simmer on low heat for 7-10 minutes.

4. At the very end you can add the coconut cream and Dijon mustard. Turn off the heat.

5. Check for seasoning and add more salt, pepper or acidity as needed. It might seem not very thick but with time it gets thicker. Serve warm with something crunchy!

Notes And Suggestions

To make the soup even thicker, simply heat it over medium heat to reduce the liquid and stir as needed until it thickens to your liking.

In order to obtain the coconut cream, chill a can of coconut milk overnight in the fridge, then turn upside down and discard the water. Use only the solid cream.

Serving size: 1 ½ cups; Calories: 250.4; Total Fat: 15.9 g; Total carbohydrate: 22.4 g; Dietary Fiber: 4.4 g; Sugars: 5.5 g; Protein: 5.7 g; Vitamin A: 1 %; Vitamin B-6: 4.4 %; Vitamin C: 9.8 %; Iron: 6 %; Calcium: 1.4 %; Magnesium: 2.2 %; Zinc: 0.8 %.

| Soups

Moroccan Style Chickpea Soup

Simple ingredients turned into a perfect combination of Moroccan flavors with chunky textures - all cooked in one pot. This soup is a filling and nutritious lunch packed with nutrient dense veggies and fibre. Serve it with a slice of gluten free bread or freshly made naan.

Course: Soup   Makes 6-7 cups   Ready in 25 minutes   GF, DF, V

INGREDIENTS

2 tbsp avocado oil (for sautéing)
1 medium onion, chopped
4 garlic cloves, minced
1 Inch fresh ginger, minced
1 ½ to 2 cup pre-cooked chickpeas (or use canned)
1 bell pepper, chopped
1 medium carrot, chopped
5 oz diced tomatoes
2 tbsp tomato paste
1 large zucchini, chopped
2 bay leaves
2 ½ - 3 cups of vegetable stock (or use chicken stock if not vegan)
1 tsp ground cumin
1/2 tsp ground coriander
1/3 tsp turmeric powder
1/4 tsp ground black pepper
salt to taste (about 1/2 tsp)
juice of ½ lemon (optional)
1 tbsp parsley, chopped, to garnish

DIRECTIONS

1. Heat a large skillet over medium-high heat with oil. Add the onion, garlic, ginger, coriander, cumin, turmeric, black pepper and cook until slightly golden.

2. Then add the chopped carrot, bell pepper, cook for about 2 minutes, then add the diced tomatoes, tomato paste adn cook for another 4-5 minutes.

3. At this point you can add the chickpeas, zucchini, bay leaves and the stock, bring to a boil then switch to low heat and simmer for about 10-15 minutes.

4. Turn off the heat. Check for seasoning and add more salt, pepper or acidity (lemon juice) if needed. Serve warm with garnished with fresh chopped parsley or cilantro.

Notes And Suggestions

If you are using dried chickpeas (garbanzo beans), soak them overnight, drain and transfer to a large cooking pot. Cover with water twice the amount of the chickpeas and bring to a boil then simmer for 1 to 2 hours.

You can make this soup without any stock as well, just use the water the chickpeas were boiled in, it will give more flavor and a thicker consistency to the soup.

Serving size: 1 ½ cups; Calories: 241.5; Total Fat: 9 g; Total carbohydrate: 35.5 g; Dietary Fiber: 9.1 g; Sugars: 10.2 g; Protein: 8 g; Vitamin A: 95.6 %; Vitamin B-6: 13.8 %; Vitamin C: 87.2 %; Iron: 6.4 %; Calcium: 6.3 %; Magnesium: 7.7 %; Zinc: 2.3 %.

Salads

• •

Turn your salad into the most delicious part of the meal. Enjoy these healthy and delicious clean eating salad recipes along with some vegan or paleo protein. Choose a crunchy or creamy texture, serve as it is, as a main meal or as an appetizer.

Tangy Watermelon Radish Salad

A mix of greens like lettuce, beet (top) greens, parsley and alfa-alfa sprouts with sliced watermelon radishes and finished with a healthy drizzle of homemade vinaigrette dressing.

Course: Salads   Serves 2   Ready in 20 minutes   GF, DF, V, P, W30

INGREDIENTS

1 large watermelon radish, thinly sliced
2 cups butter lettuce, cut into long strips
2 cups beet greens (strips) and stems
1/2 cup fresh parsley
3/4 cup alfa-alfa sprouts
1 cup sliced cucumber (optional)

Vinaigrette dressing:

1/4 cup extra virgin olive oil
3 tbsp apple cider vinegar (alternatively you can use fresh lemon juice)
2 tsp cashew butter (watermelon seed butter is a nut free alternative)
1 tsp raw honey (omit if whole30 or vegan)
1 shallot or 1 garlic clove, minced
1 tsp dried oregano
1/2 tsp sea salt
1/4 tsp black pepper

DIRECTIONS

1. In a large bowl combine the greens cut into large strips, the thinly sliced radishes, cucumber and the sprouts.

2. Combine all of the dressing ingredients in glass mason jar (or use a blender), then seal the lid and shake until the ingredients are well combined. Adjust flavor to taste, if necessary.

3. For best flavor, allow the dressing to marinate for at least 30 minutes before serving.

Notes And Suggestions

Slice the watermelon radishes thinly, either with a mandoline (preferred method) or by hand.

If you cannot find watermelon radishes, any variety of radishes can be used.

Serve immediately if you pour the dressing, otherwise the salad and the dressing can be prepared ahead of time and served later.

Serving size: half a salad: Calories: 352.3; Total Fat: 32.4 g; Total carbohydrate: 16.5 g; Protein: 4.1 g; Sugars: 6.5 g; Dietary Fiber 5.7g; Vitamin A: 94.6 %; Vitamin C: 86.2 %; Iron: 18.4 %; Calcium: 11.2 %.

Shrimp Potato Salad (Caribbean Style)

Creamy, tasty and full of flavor – dressed with a dairy free mayo "like" sauce freshly made from scratch. Serve this shrimp potato salad as a light dinner or as a side. Great for potlucks, large family gatherings, and holidays.

Course: Salads   Yields 6 cups   Ready in 1 hour   GF, DF

INGREDIENTS

1 lb medium shrimps (shelled, cooked, roughly chopped)
3 red potatoes, cooked
2 medium carrots, cooked
3 medium eggs, cooked
2 medium dill pickles
2 small celery stalks
1 red bell pepper
2 green onion stalks
fresh dill to garnish (optional)

Vegan "Mayo" dressing:

1/4 cup avocado oil
3 tbsp non dairy yogurt, unsweetened
2 tbsp white beans, cooked
2 tbsp apple cider vinegar, or lemon juice
1 tbsp stone ground mustard or Dijon mustard
1 tsp hemp seed butter – or any nut / seed butter you like
1/2 tsp sea salt
1/2 tsp onion powder
1/2 tsp arrowroot powder, optional, for thickening
1 tbsp honey or maple syrup (omit if whole30)

DIRECTIONS

1. Prepare the dressing: mix all ingredients with an immersion blender, place in the fridge to thicken for at least 1 hour before assembling the salad.

2. Chop the potatoes and carrots and cook for about 20 minutes (boil or steam) or until they are easily pierced with a fork.

3. Meanwhile, peel the shrimp and add to a saucepan with boiling water. Cook for 3 minutes. Or use pre-cooked shrimps. Just make sure they are wild and not farm raised. Also in a separate pot boil the eggs for 6-7 minutes.

4. Chop the other ingredients to a large mixing bowl (make sure they are all the same size). You can cut the shrimps or leave them whole, your choice. Once the potatoes, carrots and eggs are cool you may add them as well.

5. Toss the salad thoroughly with dressing, adding a little more if it doesn't look moist enough. Taste and add more seasonings if necessary.

Notes And Suggestions

Add more flavor and crunchiness: sprinkle some nuts, seeds or dried fruits.

Make it egg free: remove the boiled eggs. The dressing is already egg free.

Make it whole30 - remove the sweetener and the beans from the dressing and add more seed butter.

Serving size: 1 cup: Calories: 308.9; Total Fat: 15.5 g; Total carbohydrate: 18.2 g; Dietary Fiber: 2.7 g; Sugars: 5.6 g; Protein: 21.9 g; Vitamin A: 15.7 %; Vitamin B-12: 21.7 %; Vitamin B-6: 12.1 %; Vitamin C: 54.9%; Iron: 21.3 %; Calcium: 8.6 %.

Mediterranean Eggplant Salad

A chilled eggplant and bell pepper salad that is great as a side dish or as an appetizer with crackers - perfect for parties. You can also serve this hot with grilled chicken, fish or pasta.

Course: Salads   Yields 6-7 cups   Ready in 35 minutes   GF, DF, V, P, W30

INGREDIENTS

4 small eggplants (or 2 large)
4 red bell peppers
5-6 cherry tomatoes
1 med. red onion, thinly sliced
4 garlic cloves, minced
1/4 cup fresh parsley, chopped
2 tbsp olive oil
3 tbsp balsamic vinegar
dash black pepper
1 tsp salt
1 tsp basil leaves, dried

DIRECTIONS

1. Preheat oven to 400 F. Line a large sheet with parchment paper. Peel (or leave the skin for more fiber) and cut the eggplant into 2 inch strips. Cut the bell peppers the same way. Lay the eggplant and bell peppers in a single layer, drizzle with olive oil, sprinkle some salt and bake for 15 minutes. Then mix and bake again for another 10 minutes or until they start to get a nice deep brown color on the edges.

2. Heat a skillet over medium high heat and sauté the onion and garlic until slightly brown. Add the tomatoes (cut in half) at the end. Cook for 2 minutes until soft. Another option is to sear everything in a large skillet (in batches).

3. In a large bowl combine 2 tbsp olive oil, 3 tbsp balsamic vinegar, salt, basil leaves and black pepper (and 1 tbsp. maple syrup if you want it a little sweet), mix well. To that add the roasted eggplant, bell peppers, sautéed garlic, onion and tomatoes. Gently mix to combine; garnish with parsley and serve!

Notes And Suggestions

The salad tastes even better the next day. Keep it refrigerated for up to 4-5 days. For more health benefits use raw onion and garlic.

If you choose the skillet method, fry in batches so all the vegetable strips get nicely browned and not too mushy.

Fire roasted vegetables taste even better so if you have access to a grill, choose that!

Serving size: 1 cup: Calories: 119; Total Fat: 4.5 g; Total carbohydrate: 19.2 g; Dietary Fiber: 6.7 g; Sugars: 8.6 g; Protein: 3.1 g; Vitamin A: 18.6 %; Vitamin B-6: 18.9 %; Vitamin C: 120.8 %; Iron: 5.9 %; Calcium: 2.9 %; Magnesium: 10.3 %.

Fresh Spring Salad

This is a fresh crispy salad with a "creamy" dressing. Serve with barbecued meat, grilled vegetables or any other main meal. It can be easily doubled or tripled if serving a large crowd.

Course: Salads   Yields 6-7 cups   Ready in 35 minutes   GF, DF, V, P, W30

INGREDIENTS

4 cups Butter or Bibb lettuce leaves, torn
1-2 radicchio leaves, torn
1 cup red cabbage, shredded
1/2 cup green onion, chopped
1/2 cup sliced cucumber
6-7 sliced red radishes
3/4 cup fresh dill, chopped
1/4 cup homemade ranch dressing (see page 226)

DIRECTIONS

1. Toss together lettuce, radicchio, red cabbage, cucumber, radishes, onion and dill in a large salad bowl. Set aside.

2. Before serving drizzle or mix in the salad with the ranch dressing. Taste for seasonings and adjust accordingly.

Notes And Suggestions

This salad is really flexible. You could use your greens of choice instead of butter lettuce. You can also change up the chopped veggie components. Or even use other dressing.

One cup of chopped purple cabbage has 56 % of the recommended daily intake of vitamin C. It is also a great source of antioxidants that help protect against cellular damage.

The antioxidant levels in purple cabbage are around 4.5 times higher than those found in green cabbage so you better keep it in this salad.

Serving size: 1 cup: Calories: 63.6; Total Fat: 4.7 g; Total carbohydrate: 3.4 g; Dietary Fiber: 1.7 g; Sugars: 1.6 g; Protein: 0.8 g; Vitamin A: 13.6 %; Vitamin C: 28.1 %; Iron: 1.7 %; Calcium: 2.6 %; Magnesium: 1.1 %, Vitamin B-6: 1.4 %.

Creamy Beet Salad With Chicken Breast

A simple salad loaded with vitamin C that can be made in minutes when you have some leftover chicken. It's loaded with filling fiber, protein, and healthy fats, perfect to be enjoyed on its own for lunch or dinner.

Course: Salads   Yields 5-6 cups   Ready in 30 minutes   GF, DF, P, W30

INGREDIENTS

2 ½ cups steamed or roasted beets, julienned (aprox. 2 medium beet roots)
1 ½ cup chicken breast, cooked and cubed
1 medium bell peeper, chopped
20 pecan halves, chopped
1/3 cup dried cranberries, or other dried fruit
2 green onion stalks, chopped
1 large collard green leaf, chopped, or other greens
1/2 cup avocado dressing (see page 228)

DIRECTIONS

1. Steam or roast the beet roots. Julienne into fine strips.

2. Roast chicken breast (add olive oil, season with salt and pepper) in the oven for 25 minutes at 400 F. You will need about 1 large chicken breast for the recipe. Once cooled, cut into small cubes.

3. Toss together beets, chicken, green onion, bell pepper, pecans, cranberry and chopped collard greens in a large salad bowl.

4. Before serving, mix in the avocado dressing. Taste for seasonings and adjust accordingly.

Notes And Suggestions

This salad is really flexible. You could use your greens of choice. You can also change up the chopped veggie components.

Once assembled the salad will keep well in the fridge for 2-3 days. If you want to last longer, don't add the leafy greens as they degrade faster once mixed with a dressing.

Choose any other creamy dressing that you prefer.

Serving size: 1 cup: Calories: 177.4; Total Fat: 9.2 g; Total carbohydrate: 18.7 g; Dietary Fiber: 4.7 g; Sugars: 8 g; Protein: 7.2 g; Vitamin A: 11.7%; Vitamin C: 112.2 %; Iron: 7.1 %; Calcium: 3.6 %; Magnesium: 11.3 %, Vitamin B-6: 15.4 %;

| Salads

Creamy Coleslaw (Cabbage Salad)

A creamy coleslaw without mayonnaise that delivers creaminess and crunchiness with only fresh whole ingredients. It can be made year-round, served as a side-dish, on sandwiches or sliders, it's great in wraps, tacos or just as a healthy side salad for summer barbecues.

Course: Salads   Yields 6-7 cups   Ready in 20 minutes   GF, DF, V, P, W30

INGREDIENTS

Coleslaw:

5 cups white cabbage, shredded
3 cups, purple cabbage shredded
3/4 cup carrots, shredded
3 scallions, thinly sliced
3/4 cup chopped parsley

Dressing:

1 large avocado (or 2 small)
1/2 cup cashew yogurt, or coconut yogurt
1 ½ lime (the juice)
1 ½ tsp stone ground mustard
1 tbsp fresh onion, minced
1 tbsp dried dill (or fresh)
1 clove of garlic
1/3 tsp sea salt
1/2 tsp black pepper
2-3 tbsp plant milk, if it's necessary to thin it out

optional:

pinch of stevia extract, or 1 tbsp honey (if not whole30)

DIRECTIONS

1. Quarter the cabbage, remove the core and cut into thin, even shreds. You can do that with your knife or by using a mandoline slicer (which is much faster).

2. Grate the carrots by using a hand-held grater or a mandoline. Chop the greens and the scallions. Place all cut vegetables in a large bowl.

3. Make the dressing. Combine all ingredients and blend with an immersion blender until well combined and smooth.

4. Toss everything together and serve chilled.

Notes And Suggestions

This coleslaw can be made up to 4 hours in advance and refrigerated. Or you can make the dressing and cut the veggies in advance, then combine before serving.

Serving size: **1.2 cup:** Calories: 133.9; Total Fat: 8.89 g; Total carbohydrate: 11 g; Dietary Fiber: 6.36 g; Sugars: 4.4 g; Protein: 2.5 g; Vitamin A: 56.6; Vitamin B-6: 6.4 %; Vitamin C: 46.7 %; Iron: 5.1 %; Calcium: 3.6 %; Magnesium: 4.5 %.

Tangy Chickpea Salad

This salad is a quick, easy meal made with canned chickpeas and leftover food. Enjoy it in a sandwich, wrapped in a tortilla, on a bed of lettuce as a side dish or just by itself.

Course: Salads   Makes 4-5 cups   Ready in 15 minutes   GF, DF, V

INGREDIENTS

1 can (about 1 ½ cups) chickpeas, drained, rinsed
3/4 cup roasted sweet potatoes, cubed (dinner leftovers)
3/4 cup sauerkraut
3/4 cup red cabbage, shredded
1/2 sweet red pepper, chopped
2 green onion stalks
1/3 cup homemade ranch dressing (see page 226)

DIRECTIONS

1. In a large bowl toss together the chickpeas, potatoes, sauerkraut, cabbage, bell pepper and onion.

2. Pour over the homemade ranch dressing and mix until evenly coated.

Notes And Suggestions

Keep the salad in an airtight container in the fridge for up to 5-6 days.

Use sweet potatoes or white potatoes, both work well.

The tanginess of sauerkraut is essential in this salad. If you don't have any, replace it with dill pickles, capers or other ingredient with a sour taste and crunchy texture.

This salad works with any dressing, feel free to use your favorite.

Make the salad and the dressing up to a day ahead of time, store separately and combine when you are ready to serve.

Serving size: 1 cup: Calories: 147.5; Total Fat: 1.7 g; Total carbohydrate: 25.8 g; Dietary Fiber: 6.3 g; Sugars: 7.3 g; Protein: 8.5 g; Vitamin A: 16.4 %; Vitamin C: 55.6 %; Iron: 4.9 %; Calcium: 2.7 %; Vitamin B-6: 7.7 %.

Crunchy Apple Fennel Salad

Sweet and tart apples and anise-like fennel come together in a refreshingly light salad that can be prepared in just minutes. This simple crunchy salad is full of crisp textures and fresh citrus flavors. Serve it as a side to heartier dishes or by itself.

Course: Salads   Serves 4   Ready in 15 minutes   GF, DF, V, P, W30

INGREDIENTS

2 bulbs of fennel, thinly sliced
1 large crisp apple, thinly sliced
1 medium carrot, julienned
1 scallion, chopped
1 cup of greens (spring mix),
roughly chopped
1/2 cup pecans or walnuts
1/2 cup citrus vinaigrette
dressing (see page 232)

DIRECTIONS

1. Use a mandoline or a sharp knife to cut the bulb off fennel and slice in half lengthwise. Then, slice the halves as thinly as possible to create half rings. You can also slice some stalks and fronds as well.

2. Core and slice the apples too. Chop the other ingredients.

3. Combine everything in a large bowl and pour over the dressing, gently mix until evenly coated. Add the pecans at the end.

Divide salad evenly among 4 plates and serve.

Notes And Suggestions

To avoid browning, place the apple slices in the dressing (it has lemon juice) while you prepare the salad.

For beautiful, paper-thin, uniform slices use a mandoline and you'll have your salad ready in seconds.

Serving size: 1/4 of total amount: Calories: 250.7; Total Fat: 18.1 g; Total carbohydrate: 21.8 g; Dietary Fiber: 7.3 g; Sugars: 11.3 g; Protein: 3.5 g; Vitamin A: 41.5 %; Vitamin B-6: 7.6 %; Vitamin C: 40.3 %; Iron: 8.2 %; Calcium: 8.3 %; Magnesium: 11.3 %.

Mayo Free Creamy Tuna Salad

A tuna salad recipe without mayo or dairy that makes an easy quick lunch. It's also delicious on your favorite gluten free bread, crackers, wrapped in lettuce leaves or on a bed of greens.

Course: Salads   Yields 2 ½ - 3 cups   Ready in 15 minutes   GF, DF, P, W30

INGREDIENTS

1 can (5-ounce) tuna, drained
1/2 cup celery (1 stalk) finely chopped
1/3 cup green onion chopped
1/2 sweet red bell pepper, chopped
1/3 cup dried cranberries
1 boiled egg, chopped
1/2 cup homemade ranch dressing (see page 226)

DIRECTIONS

1. In a small bowl break up the tuna with a fork.

2. Add the chopped vegetables, cranberries, chopped egg and the ranch dressing. Stir to combine.

Notes And Suggestions

Keep the salad in an airtight container in the fridge for up to 4-5 days.

Add some tanginess to the salad, like sauerkraut, dill pickles, capers or other ingredient with a sour taste and crunchy texture.

The best tuna is wild caught tuna, BPA free, without added oil and fillers. I opted for Wild Planet canned tuna.

Because tuna is considered high in mercury compared to other small fishes, restrict your consumption to just once a week.

Serving size: 1.5 cup: Calories: 298.9; Total Fat: 12.4 g; Total carbohydrate: 23 g; Dietary Fiber: 3.2 g; Sugars: 14.3 g; Protein: 21.6g; Vitamin A: 16.1 %; Vitamin C: 78.7 %; Iron: 4.8 %; Calcium: 3.9 %; Vitamin B-6: 7.7 %; Magnesium: 3.3 %.

Carrot Apple Salad

A simple crisp salad full of crunch and vitamins dressed with a fresh citrus vinaigrette. This can be made during winter months as well as summer. Serve as a side dish or by itself.

Course: Salads   Yields 6-7 cups   Ready in 20 minutes   GF, DF, V, P, W30

INGREDIENTS

4 medium carrots, shredded or julienned
1 large crisp apple, shredded
1/2 small celery root, shredded
2 green onions, chopped
2-3 tbsp parsley, chopped
1/3 to 1/2 cup citrus vinaigrette dressing (see page 232)

DIRECTIONS

1. In a medium bowl, combine the prepared shredded carrots, apples, celery root and the other chopped ingredients.

2. Drizzle the dressing over the salad and toss until all of the ingredients are lightly coated in dressing. Taste and add any additional seasonings if necessary.

3. Serve immediately or cover and refrigerate for later. The lemon juice from the dressing will keep the apples from browning for at least 24 hours.

Notes And Suggestions

For the prettiest shredded carrots, use a julienne peeler or spiralizer. If you don't have one of those, a plain old box grater will work.

Feel free to add other ingredients to the salad, like seeds, nuts or dried fruit.

Serving size: 1.5 cup: Calories: 154.5; Total Fat: 7.5 g; Total carbohydrate: 21.3 g; Dietary Fiber: 4.6 g; Sugars: 9.4 g; Protein: 2.2 g; Vitamin A: 183.6 %; Vitamin B-6: 6.7 %; Vitamin C: 35 %; Iron: 3.2 %; Calcium: 6.8 %; Magnesium: 3.9 %.

Radish Dandelion & Egg Salad

A healthy salad that helps stimulate a proper digestion with a creamy anti-inflammatory dressing. Use this salad to start or finish a meal, or serve alongside your favorite dish.

Course: Salads　　　**Yields 4-5 cups**　　　**Ready in 25 minutes**　　GF, DF, P, W30

INGREDIENTS

1 ½ cup dandelion greens, chopped, tightly packed
10 red radishes, sliced
3/4 cup raw carrots, shredded or julienned
2-3 scallions, chopped
2 hard boiled eggs, chopped
3 tbsp dried cranberries

Dressing:

1/4 cup soaked cashews
1 small carrot
1/2 inch fresh ginger
1 clove of garlic
onion wedge
1/2 tsp Celtic sea salt
1/4 tsp black pepper
1/2 tsp turmeric powder
1/2 tsp Dijon mustard
1 tbsp hemp oil
2 tbsp apple cider vinegar
1 tbsp maple syrup (omit if whole30)
splash of water to thin it out, if necessary

DIRECTIONS

1. In a medium bowl, combine the prepared chopped and shredded ingredients. Set aside.

2. To prepare the dressing, mix all ingredients in a blender until creamy.

3. Drizzle the dressing over the salad and toss until all of the ingredients are lightly coated in dressing. Taste and add any additional seasonings if necessary.

4. Serve immediately or cover and refrigerate for up to 1 hour.

Notes And Suggestions

The dandelion plant is a powerful healer, it's used to purify the blood, address digestion-related problems, and prevent gallstones. It's high in vitamins A and C, and contains iron, calcium, phosphorus, potassium, magnesium and copper.

Hemp oil is rich in omega-3 fatty acid and also aids in absorption of fat soluble vitamins from the salad.

Feel free to add other ingredients to the salad, like seeds, nuts or other greens.

Serving size: 1.5 cup: Calories: 315.9; Total Fat: 23.3 g; Total carbohydrate: 32.4 g; Dietary Fiber: 6.3 g; Sugars: 15.9 g; Protein: 9.3 g; Vitamin A: 179.1 %; Vitamin B-6: 14.8 %; Vitamin C: 67.8 %; Iron: 20.3 %; Calcium: 14.9 %; Magnesium: 19.3 %; Zinc: 14.7 %.

Creamy Cucumber Summer Salad

Crisp cucumbers combined with other fresh veggies coated with a creamy avocado dressing - that feels and taste just like mayo. An easy side dish that is light, easy and perfect for a summer potluck.

Course: Salads   Yields 5 cups   Ready in 15 minutes   GF, DF, V, P, W30

INGREDIENTS

5 mini cucumbers, sliced
1 cup Romaine lettuce, shredded, tightly packed
1/2 red bell pepper
1/2 yellow bell pepper
3/4 cup celery root, shredded or julienned
2 scallions, chopped
5-6 tbsp avocado dressing (see page 228)

DIRECTIONS

1. In a medium bowl, combine the prepared chopped and shredded ingredients. Set aside.

2. Drizzle the dressing over the salad and toss until all of the ingredients are lightly coated in dressing. Taste and add any additional seasonings if necessary.

3. Serve immediately or cover and refrigerate for up to 1 hour.

Notes And Suggestions

A handful of chopped fresh dill will complement this salad beautifully!

If you don't have scallions, use red onion.

Feel free to add other ingredients to the salad, like seeds, nuts or other greens.

Serving size: 1 cup: Calories: 67.2; Total Fat: 3 g; Total carbohydrate: 10.4 g; Dietary Fiber: 2.9 g; Sugars: 2.1 g; Protein: 1.9 g; Vitamin A: 10.2 %; Vitamin B-6: 6.8 %; Vitamin C: 128.8 %; Iron: 3.8 %; Calcium: 3.8 %; Magnesium: 4.9 %; Zinc: 2.4 %.

Desserts

· ·

Sweet cakes, pies, cookies and pastries made without dairy, refined gluten free flours or refined sugar. There is no refined oils or cheap nutritionless vegan butters - margarine, only wholesome clean ingredients. Perfect for birthdays or any occasion that calls for a celebration.

Lazy Cinnamon Roll Cake

All of the flavors you love from a cinnamon roll, in a delicious, easy, moist cake without any of the fuss. No yeast, no rising time, it's simple to put together and creates a dessert that melts in your mouth.

Course: Dessert   Makes 8 large slices   Ready in 35 minutes   GF, DF

INGREDIENTS

Cake batter:

2 large eggs
1/2 cup plant milk
1/2 cup plant yogurt (plain)
1/3 cup melted vegan butter
1/2 maple sugar (or other sweetener)
2 ¼ cup lightweight flour blend (see page 272)
2 tbsp ground flax seeds (golden)
3/4 tsp baking soda
1 tsp lemon juice
1 tsp vanilla extract
pinch of salt

Cinnamon swirls:

8 medjool dates (soaked, pitted)
1/3 cup coconut sugar
1/4 cup melted vegan butter
3 tsp cinnamon powder
3/4 cup cake batter, made earlier

Icing:

4 tbsp coconut condensed milk
2 tbsp plant milk, of your choice

DIRECTIONS

1. Preheat oven to 350°F (175°C) and line, or very lightly oil, a 9 inch (deep) round baking dish (3 quart). Or use a rectangular 9x13-inch baking dish.

2. **Prepare the cake batter**. In a large bowl, whisk together milk, eggs, yogurt, sugar and vanilla extract. Then add the flour, ground flax seeds and salt, mix until mostly incorporated. At the end whisk in melted butter. Mix in (gently) the baking soda when the cinnamon swirl is ready, to immediately assemble and bake.

3. **Prepare the cinnamon swirl.** Soak the dates in hot water for easier peeling and for softening. Then mix them with the rest of ingredients in a blender until smooth. At the end mix in 3/4 cup of the prepared cake batter and give it a gentle mix so you don't disperse the bubbles much.

4. Pour half of the cake batter into the baking dish. Drop spoonfuls of cinnamon mixture on the batter, using half of the topping. Use the tip of a butter knife to swirl the topping through the cake. Pour the rest of the batter on top and spoon the rest of the cinnamon topping on and swirl again.

5. Bake for 35 minutes. Remove from oven and let cool.

6. **Prepare the icing.** Whisk together the coconut condensed milk with 2-3 tbsp of plant milk to get a pourable texture. Drizzle cake with frosting. Cut and serve!

Serving size: 1 slice (without icing): Calories: 385.7; Total Fat: 18.9 g; Total carbohydrate: 62 g; Protein: 6.1 g; Sugars: 25.9 g; Dietary Fiber: 5.9 g; Vitamin A: 1.5; Vitamin C: 1.6 %; Iron: 4.3 %; Calcium: 6.1 %; Vitamin B-12: 2%; Vitamin B-6: 6.9%.

Pecan Stuffed Prunes In Chocolate

Chewy tangy prunes (plums) stuffed with crunchy pecans and coated with dairy free melted chocolate. The healthiest chocolate treat or snack you can have that also improves digestion.

Course: Dessert   Makes 15 stuffed prunes   Ready in 20 minutes   GF, DF, V

INGREDIENTS

15 dried prunes
6 oz dairy free chocolate chips, melted
15 pecans, halves
2 tbsp coconut oil (optional, for thinning out the chocolate)

DIRECTIONS

1. Insert the pecans (or other preferred nut) into the centers of the prunes, one nut per prune. Find the small hole that was used to take out the pits for inserting the nut.

2. Gently melt your chocolate and coconut oil in a double boiler stirring continuously until melted. Not directly in the pot. Chocolate should be fluid and barely warm. Remove from heat.

3. Add your prunes (in batches) to the chocolate and toss well, ensuring that all of the prunes are well coated. Or dip one at a time.

4. Line a small baking sheet with parchment paper. Separate the prunes one by one and put them on the parchment paper.

5. Let the chocolate set until hard again. Enjoy!

Notes and Suggestions

Coconut oil is used to make the chocolate more shiny and thinner but you can leave it out if you want less fat.

Alternative fillings: almonds, peanuts, walnuts or nut butters.

Store the chocolate prunes in an airtight container in the refrigerator for up to 10 days.

Serving size: 1 chocolate prune: Calories: 92; Total Fat: 5.4 g; Total carbohydrate: 12.4 g; Protein: 1.1 g; Sugars: 8.5 g; Dietary Fiber: 1.5 g; Vitamin A: 1.3 %; Vitamin C: 0.1 %; Iron: 5.2%; Calcium: 2%.

Peach Galette

A rustic summer dessert made of a pie dough wrapped around fresh peaches. It's easy to make and it doesn't require a special pan - just a nice flat surface.

Course: Dessert   Makes 8 slices   Ready in 1 hour   GF, DF, V

INGREDIENTS

Crust:

1 ½ cup lightweight flour blend (see page 272)
1 tbsp flax meal
1 tbsp psyllium husk
1/2 cup vegan butter, frozen cubes
pinch of salt
4 tbsp water, cold
1 tbsp apple cider vinegar
1/2 tsp baking soda
2 tbsp maple sugar

Filling:

5-6 medium peaches, cubed 1/2 cup maple sugar
2 tbsp arrowroot flour
juice of half a lemon
1/2 tsp cardamom
1/2 tsp cinnamon
1/3 cup sliced almonds, as topping

DIRECTIONS

1. Make the filling. Peel and cut the peaches into cubes. Add ingredients for the filling into a pan and cook for 3-4 min until the juice is gelatinized. Set aside to cool.

2. Form the crust. In a small bowl add the cold water, apple cider vinegar, salt, sugar, flax meal (super fine) and psyllium husk, mix and let it gelatinize.

Meanwhile in the bowl of a food processor add the dry ingredients + vegan butter, "pulse" several times until the butter has disappeared into the flour. Then add the gelatinized composition, and with a few more pulses the dough starts to come together. If it still looks too wet, add 1 - 2 tbsp of more flour. Form a ball with your hands. Then use a rolling pin to make a thin pie crust between two parchment papers (picture 1). Once the crust is rolled out, let the dough chill for 5 minutes in the freezer. Preheat the oven to 400F.

3. Assemble and bake. Place the rolled crust on a flat baking sheet. Remove the top parchment paper and place the peach filling in the middle, spread it leaving enough room to fold the edges. Fold over the excess dough (together with parchment paper) covering the outer edge of the filling (picture 2). Sprinkle with sliced almonds, some maple sugar (optional). Bake for 20 minutes at 400F, and another 25 minutes at 370F. Retrieve from the oven. Let it cool. Slice and serve!

Notes and Suggestions

Make sure to use very cold water and butter for the best results. Feel free to use any fruits of your choice, just make sure the filling is not too wet when assembled.

Serving size: 1 slice: Calories: 268.1; Total Fat: 13.4 g; Total carbohydrate: 35.4 g; Protein: 3.5 g ; Sugars: 9.3 g; Dietary Fiber: 5 g; Vitamin A: 7.9 %; Vitamin C: 10.1 %; Iron: 4.6 %; Calcium: 3.2 %; Magnesium: 4.6 %; Zinc: 3.8 %.

Chocolate Chip Cookies

Soft and chewy chocolate chip cookies with a slight crunch on the outside and loaded with semi-sweet chocolate chips. Made healthier without refined sugar, dairy or gluten.

Course: Dessert   Makes 15-17 cookies   Ready in 30 minutes   GF, DF

INGREDIENTS

1 ½ cup lightweight flour blend
(see page 272)
1/3 tsp baking soda
1/6 tsp salt
1/2 cup vegan butter
1 cup coconut sugar (or maple
sugar)
1 egg
1 tsp vanilla extract
3/4 cup dairy free semi-sweet
chocolate chips
or semi-sweet chocolate chunks
(chopped)

DIRECTIONS

1. Preheat oven to 350 F, line a cookie sheet with parchment paper.

2. In a bowl with an electric mixer, beat the vegan butter (melted - yogurt like consistency), and sugar – about 2 minutes then add the egg (room temperature) and vanilla, mix until combined.

3. Add baking soda, salt and the flour, mixing until you get a dough like consistency. It will look a bit runnier than normal. Therefore you will need to chill the dough for at least 30-40 min. The flour will absorb more liquid and it will get thicker. Then fold in the chocolate chips.

4. Using an ice cream scoop (about 1.5 tbsp), drop balls of dough onto cookie sheet, place them about 2" apart, they are going to spread a lot.

5. Bake for exactly 11 minutes. Allow to cool for about 10 minutes before transferring to a cooling rack. They are pretty fragile at first, once fully cooled they get sturdier.

Notes And Suggestions

Do not over-bake! When you remove the cookies from the oven they will look slightly underdone. But they are ready! This is what makes the cookies chewy. If you wait for them to turn brown they will turn drier and crispier.

If you don't want fluffy cookies make sure you use room temperature ingredients and melted butter. Too much flour will result in thicker cake-like cookies.

Serving size: 1 cookie: Calories: 179.3; Total Fat: 8.2 g; Total carbohydrate: 26.4 g; Protein: 1.9 g; Sugars: 15.9 g; Dietary Fiber: 1.2g; Vitamin A: 0.4 %; Vitamin B-6: 1.7 %; Vitamin C: 0 %; Calcium: 1.4 %; Iron: 4.8 %; Magnesium 1.1 %, Zinc: 0.9 %.

Carob "Chocolate" Chip Cookies

Soft and delicious cookies with chocolaty flavor due to carob. These cookies are vegan, gluten free and a perfect treat for those allergic to chocolate.

Course: Dessert   Makes 12 large cookies   Ready in 35 minutes   GF, DF, V

INGREDIENTS

1 ½ cup apple sauce
1/2 cup coconut cream
1/2 cup coconut sugar (or other sweetener)
3/4 cup teff flour
1/2 cup carob powder (or cacao, if not allergic)
1/3 cup green banana flour
1 cup carob chips (or chocolate chips)
3 tbsp ground flax seeds
1 tsp baking soda
1 tsp lemon juice
1 tsp vanilla extract
1/4 tsp Himalayan pink salt

DIRECTIONS

1. Set the oven to 360 F and line with parchment paper a large baking sheet.

2. In a large bowl combine the apple sauce the coconut cream (room temperature), sugar, vanilla extract and the ground flax seeds. Mix well and let the seeds absorb the liquid for 10 minutes.

3. Then add the rest of ingredients. Mix to combine but do not overmix.

4. Scoop approximately 1.5 tbsp of dough onto prepared cookie sheet, about 2 inches apart.

5. Bake for 25 minutes or just until they don't seem soft to the touch. Transfer to a cooling rack to cool completely.

Notes And Suggestions

Carob comes from a carob tree, which grows basically fruit pods and is often used as a healthy chocolate alternative.

The carob chips look exactly like chocolate chips, but they have a more nuttier flavor.

Find carob chips online. If you're not allergic to chocolate you can swap the carob powder and chips to cocoa powder and regular dairy free chocolate chips.

Bake immediately after you mix in the baking soda or else the mixture will collapse.

Serving size: 1 cookie: Calories: 120.3; Total Fat: 2 g; Total carbohydrate: 22.3 g; Protein: 3.9 g; Sugars: 9.5 g; Dietary Fiber: 2 g; Vitamin A: 0; Vitamin C: 1.9 %; Iron: 0.9 %; Calcium: 2.6%.

Buckwheat And Oat Cookies

Soft inside with a slight crunch on the outside these buckwheat cookies are easy to make and are perfect as a snack, light dessert or breakfast on to go. They are naturally sweetened with fruit and don't require added sugar.

Course: Dessert   Makes 18 cookies   Ready in 50 minutes   GF, DF, V

INGREDIENTS

1 cup buckwheat flour
1 cup rolled oats, gluten free
1 large apple, grated (about 1 cup tightly packed)
1 cup apple sauce
1 banana, mashed
6 dates, soaked to soften and pitted
1 tsp cinnamon
1/3 tsp cardamom
1/2 tsp baking soda
1/8 tsp salt

DIRECTIONS

1. Preheat oven to 375 F, line a cookie sheet with parchment paper. Soak the dates in warm water at least 10 minutes before mixing the ingredients.

2. In a bowl mix the dry ingredients, set aside. In a separate bowl combine the mashed banana, apple sauce and the grated apples. Dice the dates and add to the mixture. Then add the dry ingredients. Mix to combine. If the mixture looks too dry, add 2-3 tablespoons of water. The dough should look like a thick oatmeal porridge.

3. Using an ice cream scoop (about 1.5 tbsp), drop balls of dough onto cookie sheet, place them about 0.5 inch apart (they will not spread) and flatten with your hand or a fork.

4. Bake for 40-45 minutes. Allow to cool for about 10 minutes before transferring to a cooling rack. To develop a solid brown crust you might need to bake them a bit longer in the oven, otherwise these cookies will be on the soft side.

Notes And Suggestions

Add seeds or nuts if you want. If you don't have buckwheat flour you can easily make it by grinding the buckwheat groats in a blender.

If you don't like dates, you can swap them for other dried fruits.

Serving size: 2 cookies: Calories: 160.6; Total Fat: 1.1 g; Total carbohydrate: 37.3 g; Protein: 3.3 g; Sugars: 16.7 g; Dietary Fiber: 4.7g; Vitamin A: 0.9 %; Vitamin B-6: 4.4 %; Vitamin C: 4.8 %; Iron: 7.4 %; Calcium: 1.8 %, Magnesium: 2.7 %.

Layered Apple Dump Cake

A slightly different dump cake where the dry ingredients are layered with shredded apples and baked into a soft cake with a crispy crust - perfect for fall and with a cup of hot tea.

Course: Dessert   Makes 12 slices   Ready in 1 h 15 minutes   GF, DF, V

INGREDIENTS

Prepare the apples:

8 medium apples, thinly sliced, or chopped
1/2 tsp cinnamon
1/2 tsp cardamom
juice of one large lemon

Dry ingredients:

3/4 cup whole millet
1 cup lightweight flour blend (see page 272)
1 cup maple sugar or other sweetener
1/4 tsp pink salt
1 tsp baking soda
8 oz vegan butter, frozen

Topping:

1 cup chopped walnuts, or pecans
2 tbsp maple sugar

DIRECTIONS

1. Place the butter in the freezer 20 minutes before baking. Set the oven to 360 F and prepare a 9x13 inch pan.

2. In a food processor coarsely ground the millet (it should resemble the granulated sugar texture) then transfer in a bowl and combine with the rest of dry ingredients. Divide this mixture in 3 portions.

3. Prepare the apples: core and coarsely chop up in the same food processor (or grate). Mix in the lemon juice, maple sugar, cinnamon and cardamom. Stir until completely combined. Divide in 3 portions.

4. For assembling: grate 1/4 cup of butter on the bottom of the pan, follow with a layer of flour mixture, then a layer of apples. Repeat with a layer of dry flour mixture, a layer of grated butter and then a layer of apples. And again: flour mixture, butter and apples, top with chopped walnuts and a sprinkle of maple sugar to caramelize them.

5. Bake for about 45 minutes. Cool completely, until it sets. Or serve slightly warm.

Notes And Suggestions

Keep leftovers covered in the refrigerator up to 3 days.

Can't find millet? Use coarse almond flour or rolled oats.

Add another thin layer of grated butter on top if you like.

Use a smaller pan if you want the cake to look taller.

Serving size: 1 slice: Calories: 355.3; Total Fat: 20.5 g; Total carbohydrate: 43.2 g; Protein: 2.8 g; Sugars: 26.2 g; Dietary Fiber: 5 g; Vitamin A: 1.4 %; Vitamin C: 7 %; Iron: 5.3 %; Calcium: 4.2 %; Magnesium: 9.7 %; Zinc: 9.8 %.

Oatmeal Blueberry Peach Cookies

Healthy oatmeal cookies full of juicy fresh blueberries, peach and maple flavor, with a crispy crust and chewy inside. Because of their clean ingredients, they are more like a healthy snack than regular sugary cookies.

Course: Dessert   Makes 14-15 cookies   Ready in 55 minutes   GF, DF, V

INGREDIENTS

2 cups rolled oats (soaked)
1 cup apple sauce
3/4 cup tigernut flour, or almond flour, or any seed flour
1/3 cup freshly ground golden flax seeds
1/3 cup oil (like avocado oil)
1 fresh large peach, cubed
3/4 cup fresh blueberries
pinch stevia extract powder (or use 3-4 tbsp maple sugar)
pinch of salt
1/2 tsp baking soda
1/2 tsp lemon juice
1/4 cup maple sugar, for sprinkling
Video recipe also available on the blog.

DIRECTIONS

1. Preheat the oven to 360 F, and line a large baking sheet with parchment paper.

2. Whisk together the apple sauce, the oil and ground flax seeds. In a separate bowl, whisk together the oats (soaked for 10-15 min), tigernut flour, salt, stevia extract (use maple sugar or coconut sugar if you prefer them sweet). Mix the wet ingredients with dry ingredients, stirring just until incorporated. At the end add baking soda + lemon juice to create leavening, give it a final gentle mix to incorporate.

3. Using a spoon and spatula, drop the cookie dough (scoops) onto the prepared sheet. Add the peach (small chunks) and blueberries on top. Sprinkle with maple sugar or coconut sugar. This will create a sweet crunchy crust.

4. Bake at 360 F for 35-40 minutes. Cool on the pan for 10 minutes before turning out onto a wire rack to cool completely.

Notes And Suggestions

Vanilla extract may be added.

Make sure to prepare (cube) the fruits first, before putting together the dough. Once you mixed baking soda and the acid you need to bake the cookies immediately. Otherwise they will not puff up. If you want your cookies crispier, don't soak the oats and bake for 10 min longer.

Fruits that are frozen will work too (only make sure there is no extra liquid).

Serving size: 1 cookie: Calories: 142.3; Total Fat: 7.9 g; Total carbohydrate: 16.64 g; Protein: 2.4 g; Sugars: 4.35 g; Dietary Fiber: 4.4 g; Vitamin A: 1.5%; Vitamin C: 3.3 %; Iron: 3.9%; Calcium: 0.5 %; Zinc 0.6 %.

Maple Coconut Macaroons With Chocolate

Classic coconut macaroons with a subtle maple vanilla flavor made with healthy, whole ingredients and drizzled with melted chocolate - crisp on the outside with a moist interior.

Course: Dessert   Yields 15-16 macaroons   Ready in 35 min   GF, DF, P

INGREDIENTS

4 egg whites
2 cups shredded coconut (unsweetened)
1/3 cup maple sugar
1/6 tsp salt
1 tsp vanilla extract
3 tbsp vegan butter (melted - for a softer interior)

Chocolate drizzle:

2 oz melted semi-sweet dairy free chocolate chips
2 tbsp plant milk (for thinning)

Video recipe also available on the blog.

DIRECTIONS

1. Heat oven to 350 F. Line a baking sheet with parchment paper.

2. Whisk the eggs whites (cold) in a large bowl with an electric mixer on medium-high until soft peaks form, 2 to 3 minutes. Add vanilla and salt. With the machine running slowly add the maple sugar until dissolved and the egg white mixture becomes stiff (just like a meringue).

3. Fold in the melted butter (not hot) and the coconut shreds, gently stir to combine.

4. Using a small ice cream scoop, drop the batter in mounds 1 inch apart on the prepared baking sheet. Bake, until golden brown, approximately 18-20 minutes; let cool completely.

5. In a double boiler on the stove, melt the chocolate chips with 2 tbsp plant milk stirring until smooth. Drizzle the chocolate on top of the macaroons.

Notes And Suggestions:

There is a lot of variability in coconut depending on the brand you purchase, make sure the final "dough" is not too wet (there shouldn't be anything dripping) nor too dry, adjust accordingly.

You can also use coconut condensed milk (1/4 cup) add it after you get a stiff egg white mixture and leave out the maple sugar.

The macaroons will keep for up to 5 days (room temperature) in an airtight container. They can be frozen for up to 3 months.

Serving size: 1 coconut macaroon (no chocolate): Calories: 127; Total Fat: 10.3 g; Total carbohydrate: 8.4 g; Protein: 2 g; Sugars: 5.7 g; Dietary Fiber: 1.6 g; Vitamin A: 0 %; Vitamin C: 0 %; Iron: 0.5 %; Calcium: 0.5 %.

Crunchy Grain Free Apple Crisp

A delicious vegan, paleo apple crisp with maple and pecan flavor. An easy apple crisp recipe made with tons of honey crisp apples and a crunchy, flavorful crumble topping.

Course: Dessert   Makes 8 servings   Ready in 1 hour   GF, DF, V, P

INGREDIENTS

Prepare the apples:

5 large or 6 medium apples, sliced
1 ½ tsp cinnamon
1/4 tsp nutmeg
1/4 tsp cardamom
juice of half a lemon
3 tbsp maple syrup or sugar (or other sweetener)
1 tbsp arrowroot powder (optional, for absorbing the juices)
1/6 tsp Himalayan pink salt

Prepare the topping:

3/4 cup tigernut flour (or some other nut flour)
3/4 cup pecans or walnuts
4 tbsp golden flax seeds (ground)
3 tbsp maple syrup
6 tbsp coconut butter (melted, or vegan butter)
1 tsp vanilla extract
1/6 tsp Himalayan pink salt
1 tsp cinnamon
1/4 tsp nutmeg
4 tbsp sliced tigernuts, or sliced almonds (optional, for visual presentation)

DIRECTIONS

1. Set the oven to 350 F and grease a 9x13 inch pan.

2. In a large bowl combine sliced apples, lemon juice, maple syrup (or maple sugar), arrowroot powder, tigernut flour (is nut free, or use almond flour), cinnamon, nutmeg, cardamom, salt and vanilla. Stir until completely combined. Place the apples in the pan, distribute evenly.

3. For the topping, place all ingredients in a food processor (except tigernut slices) and pulse a few times until you get a thick, crumbly mixture. Add the tigernut slices to the mixture and sprinkle evenly over the apple mixture.

4. Bake the apple crisp covered with a foil for 15 minutes then remove the foil and bake for 30 minutes until the fruit is bubbling and the topping is golden brown and crisp. Since the nuts may brown quicker the foil will prevent that.

5. Serve warm with a non dairy ice cream if desired.

Notes And Suggestions

Best apples to use: Honeycrisp and Granny Smith. Be sure to slice your apples thinly so they become fully tender.

The crisp is best when fresh, though leftovers keep covered in the refrigerator up to 3 days, or in the freezer up to 1 month.

Serving size: 1 cup; Calories: 335.5; Total Fat: 17.9 g; Total carbohydrate: 46.2 g; Protein: 5.6 g; Sugars: 28.2 g; Dietary Fiber: 13.4 g; Vitamin A: 0%; Vitamin C: 5.2 %; Iron: 5.2 %; Calcium: 5.7 %.

The Ultimate Coffee Sponge Cake

Airy, sponge-like and so soft, this layered cake with chocolate notes is complemented with a rich coffee flavored frosting. A delicious luxurious dessert for coffee lovers!

Course: Dessert   Makes 6 large square slices   Ready in 2 hours   GF, DF

INGREDIENTS

Cake batter:

6 large eggs
1 cup coconut sugar, or maple sugar
1 ¼ cup lightweight flour blend (see page 272)
3 tbsp cacao powder
1 tsp baking soda
1 tsp apple cider vinegar
1/6 tsp sea salt

Soaking liquid:

2/3 cup hot water
1 tbsp instant decaf coffee
1 tbsp maple syrup
1 tsp cacao powder

Frosting:

8 oz vegan butter
13 oz coconut whipping cream
2 tbsp instant decaf coffee
3/4 cup maple sugar (powdered)
To make the powder, just place the maple sugar and coffee in a blender and mix on high speed until finely powdered.
3 oz semi-sweet chocolate chunks (melted)

DIRECTIONS

1. Preheat oven to 360 F. Line a baking sheet (mine is 16.5"x11") with parchment paper. Set aside.

2. Make the cake batter: In a large bowl, using a hand mixer, beat the eggs and coconut sugar on high speed for about 8 minutes, until thick, fluffy and the volume triples.

3. Sift the flours, salt and cacao powder and gradually fold into batter, then add the baking soda and apple cider vinegar, mix gently, just enough to incorporate everything. If you mix too much the mixture will lose its bubbles. Pour the batter into the baking sheet. Bake for 13-15 minutes without opening the oven.

4. Let cool for a minute then release the edges from baking sheet / paper, then place a large cutting board on top and flip it over. Gently peel off the entire parchment paper. Set aside to cool completely.

5. Prepare the frosting: let the vegan butter soften a bit at room temperature. Meanwhile whip the coconut cream (it should be chilled for at least 2-3 hours). Mix the butter with maple sugar plus instant coffee - both powdered, (add gradually) until creamy. Then fold in the whipped coconut cream, little by little until fully incorporated. Chill before decorating if it gets too liquidy.

6. Assemble the cake: Cut the cake into 4 (picture 1), so you get smaller rectangles. Place the first layer on a serving plate, pour over a few tablespoons of soaking liquid, then proceed with a generous layer of frosting, repeat until you finish with last layer. Cover the sides with the remaining frosting. Dust with cacao powder and drizzle with melted chocolate (picture 2).

7. Let it set and cool in the fridge for at least 5-6 hours, then cut and serve. Will keep refrigerated for up to 4-5 days, or freeze.

Serving size: 1 slice (36 oz): Calories: 710.6; Total Fat: 32 g; Total carbohydrate: 89.2 g; Protein: 18 g; Sugars: 59.6 g; Dietary Fiber: 2.7 g; Vitamin A: 5.3 %; Vitamin B-6: 7.9%; Vitamin B-12:7 %; Vitamin C: 0 %; Iron: 10.6 %; Calcium: 4.2 %; Zinc: 13.1 %.

175

Eclairs With Custard Filling (Pastry Cream)

Gluten free and dairy free pastry made with choux dough filled with vanilla pastry cream and topped with chocolate icing. They're light and airy and they puff up in the middle when baked. You can use the same dough and filling to make cream puffs!

Course: Dessert   Makes 12 eclairs   Ready in 1 h 30 minutes   GF, DF

INGREDIENTS

Choux pastry dough:

8 tbsp vegan butter

1 cup plant milk (coconut)

1 cup lightweight flour blend (see page 272)

1/2 tsp psyllium husk

3 large eggs

1 tbsp maple sugar (or other granulated sweetener)

1/4 tsp sea salt

Pastry cream:

1 ½ cups plant milk

6 tbsp maple sugar (or other granulated sweetener)

4 egg yolks

3 tbsp arrowroot powder

3 tbsp vegan butter

1 teaspoon vanilla extract

pinch of salt

Chocolate glaze:

4 oz semisweet dairy free chocolate chunks

1/3 cup coconut cream

DIRECTIONS

1. Make the pastry cream first. In a saucepan, warm the milk over low heat until it is just hot enough to steam. While the milk is warming, whisk together the egg yolks, sugar, arrowroot powder, salt and vanilla until the mixture is thick and smooth. Remove the milk from heat. Slowly pour half, in a thin stream, into the egg mix, while whisking constantly. Then add the egg mix back into the hot milk in the saucepan. Heat it, over medium heat, whisking until it starts to thicken (about 1-2 minutes). Remove from heat, stir in the vegan butter, and chill, then place in the fridge to set.

2. Make the choux pastry. Preheat oven to 400 F. Place the milk, butter, salt and sugar in a saucepan and heat until it comes to a boil, stirring occasionally. When is almost boiling add the psyllium husk, stir until dissolves, remove from the heat and add the flour.

Using a silicone spatula, stir until a sticky batter is formed (like a playdough). Return the pan to the stove and let it cook until you see a film of dough forming on the bottom of the pan. Transfer the dough into a bowl. Flatten it along the wall of the bowl, to cool for 5-6 min. Next add the eggs (room temperature) 1 at a time, mix until the batter is smooth (use a mixer). The dough should look glossy and pipe-able.

Place it in a pastry bag with a French star tip. Pipe the eclairs (4 - 5 inches in length) on a lined baking tray.

Bake in the oven for 25 minutes then, turn down to 375 F, prick each of the eclairs with a skewer on the ends to release the steam and bake for another 5-8 minutes. Open slightly the door and allow them to sit in the oven (turned off) until dry (~ 30 minutes).

3. Make the chocolate glaze. Place the chocolate chips in a large bowl and pour the hot (almost boiling) cream on top, stir until melted.

4. Assemble the eclairs. Transfer the pastry cream to a pastry bag with a small round tip, make 3 holes on the bottom of each eclair shell and fill through these holes. Then dip each in the chocolate glaze. Sprinkle with crushed nuts (optional), allow to set and serve! They keep well for 2 days, then they start to get soggy.

Serving size: 1 eclair: Calories: 225.8; Total Fat: 15.3; Total carbohydrate: 19.1; Protein: 4.1; Sugars: 6.4; Dietary Fiber: 1.2 g; Vitamin A: 3.2 %; Vitamin C: 1.2 %; Iron: 12.7 %; Calcium: 2.5 %.

Grain Free Chocolate Coffee Cake

This chocolate coffee cake with walnuts and dates is so easy to make and is moist and rich, just like a brownie. A blend of coffee and chocolate, flavored with vanilla, no frosting needed - perfect for a large crowd as dessert.

Course: Dessert   Makes 8 large slices   Ready in 1 hour   GF, DF, P

INGREDIENTS

1 cup strong coffee or essspresso
1 cup plant milk
4 cups grain free flour mix (see page 278)
1/4 cup cocoa powder
1/2 cup vegan butter, melted, or oil
1 ½ cup maple sugar or coconut sugar
2 large eggs
1 ½ cup walnuts, coarsely chopped
2 cups dates, chopped (soaked) or dried prunes
1 ½ tsp baking soda
1 tsp cinnamon powder
1/2 tsp cardamom (optional)
1/4 tsp sea salt
1 tbsp vanilla extract

DIRECTIONS

1. Preheat oven to 350 F. Grease (or cover with parchment paper) a 9x9 inch square pan.

2. Soak the dried dates (or prunes) in hot water for 15 minutes, remove pits, and chop. Set aside.

3. Add wet ingredients into a bowl (coffee - warm, plant milk (warm), melted vegan butter, vanilla and eggs - room temperature, give everything a good mix until frothy. Use a mixer if you want to do it faster.

4. In the same bowl add the maple sugar, mix until incorporated then add the flour, baking soda, cinnamon, cardamom and salt.

5. Fold in the walnuts and the chopped dates. Pour the batter into the prepared pan and bake for 35-40 minutes or until a toothpick inserted near the center of the cake comes out clean.

Notes And Suggestions

Technically, coffee isn't acceptable on paleo diet but many still use it while in transition. Furthermore, coffee is potentially cross-reactive with gluten so make sure you're ok with it first.

Coffee enhances the chocolate flavor but you can skip it, just use more milk instead. If you want, glaze it with some chocolate sauce.

You can also replace the flour with your favorite. Freeze it for up to 3 months. Thaw in the fridge overnight before serving.

Serving size: 1 slice (3" square): Calories: 667.5; Total Fat: 31.9 g; Total carbohydrate: 106.1 g; Protein: 9.9 g; Sugars: 63.6 g; Fiber: 8.4 g; Vitamin A: 3 %; Vitamin B-6: 12.7 %; Vitamin C: 0.6 %; Iron: 14.4 %; Calcium: 12.2 %; Magnesium: 22.7 %.

Easy Moist Apple Nut Cake

A tender flavorful cake, simple and easy to make, featuring walnuts, apples and cinnamon. The perfect combination of aromas to be enjoyed with a cup of tea. You'll love how effortlessly this recipe comes together.

Course: Dessert   Makes 6 slices   Ready in 55 minutes   GF, DF, V

INGREDIENTS

2 medium apples, finely chopped
1 ¼ cup flour blend no. 1 or no. 2 (see page 274)
1/4 cup flavorless oil (or vegan butter, melted)
1/2 cup dairy free yogurt, unsweetened
3/4 cup maple sugar (or coconut sugar)
1 ½ tbsp lemon juice
1 large egg
1 cup walnuts, finely chopped
1 tsp baking soda
3/4 tsp cinnamon powder
1/2 tsp cardamom
1/4 tsp sea salt

DIRECTIONS

1. Preheat oven to 350 F. Grease (or cover with parchment paper) a 9x9 inch square pan.

2. Prepare the apples: if you want them ready quickly, use a food processor in order to get a coarse chop, push and immediately release the pulse button about 3-4 times. Add lemon juice, cinnamon, cardamom and mix to coat evenly. Set aside.

3. Beat the egg and sugar with an electric mixer on high speed until the sugar dissolves and puffs up. Then add the butter and yogurt, mix to combine. Then add the flour, salt and give everything a good mix again. Use a mixer if you want to do it faster.

4. Fold in the apples and nuts. At the end add the baking soda and give a final gentle mix with a spatula. Pour the batter into the prepared pan and bake for 50 minutes or until a toothpick inserted near the center of the cake comes out clean.

5. The cake is very light and tender when it's warm, let it cool completely before slicing it will firm up. Dust with powdered maple sugar or powdered freeze dried fruits.

Notes And Suggestions

Vanilla extract may be added.

Make sure to prepare (cube) the fruits first, before putting together the dough. Once you mixed baking soda and the acid you need to bake the cookies immediately. Otherwise they will not puff up. If you want your cookies crispier, don't soak the oats and bake for 10 min longer.

Fruits that are frozen will work too (only make sure there is no extra liquid).

Serving size: 1 slice: Calories: 560.5; Total Fat: 43.6 g; Total carbohydrate: 38.1 g; Protein: 6.6 g; Sugars: 15.7 g; Fiber: 5 g; Vitamin A: 1 %; Vitamin B-6: 0.8 %; Vitamin C: 0.3 %; Iron: 2.8 %; Calcium: 4.9 %; Magnesium: 8.9 %, Zinc: 3.9 %.

Dutch Apple Pie

A vegan gluten free pie crust with layers of cinnamon scented baked apples, finished with a sweet and crunchy crumble / streusel topping. Perfect as dessert to your holiday table.

Course: Dessert   Makes 8 slices   Ready in 1 h 10 minutes   GF, DF, V

INGREDIENTS

Pie crust:

1/2 cup oat flour
1/2 cup cassava flour
1/3 cup sorghum flour
1 ½ tbsp ground flax seeds +
3 tbps of water (to make a flax "egg")
6 tbsp cold vegan butter
2-3 tbsp maple sugar
3 tbsp filtered water, cold
1/3 tsp baking soda
1/2 tsp apple cider vinegar, or lemon juice

Pie filling:

6 medium apples
1 ½ tbsp lemon juice
1/2 cup maple sugar
3 tbsp arrowroot powder, to absorb the juice
1/2 tsp cinnamon
1/3 tsp nutmeg

Crumble topping:

1/4 cup rolled oats, gluten free
1/3 cup walnuts, or pecans
3 tbsp cassava flour
1/4 cup maple sugar
5 tbsp vegan butter
pinch of salt

DIRECTIONS

1. Make the pie filling. Peel and cut the apples into thin slices. Add ingredients for the filling into a pan and cook for 5 min with a splash of water until the juice is gelatinized. Set aside to cool.

2. Form the crust. In the bowl of a food processor add the dry ingredients + vegan butter, "pulse" several times until the butter has disappeared into the flour. Then add the apple cider vinegar, the flax "egg", the water and with a few more pulses the dough starts to come together. Form a ball with your hands.

Lay a large sheet of parchment paper on your counter and place the ball of dough on it. Press down with your hands to start to flatten out the ball. Then use a rolling pin to make a thin pie crust. Once the crust is rolled out, carefully place the baking dish on top and flip it over. Gently lower the crust into your pie pan and remove the parchment paper. I used a 9" diameter glass dish with walls. Adjust the crust. Make sure to leave some dough at the edge to form a short "wall". Prick the bottom of the crust all over with a fork. Bake at 390 F for 15-18 minutes.

3. Make the crumble topping. Combine all ingredients in the same bowl you made the pie crust. Pulse a few times until crumbs are formed. Place in the refrigerator to keep cool.

4. Assemble and bake. Retrieve the pie crust from the oven. Pour the baked apples on top, arrange them then sprinkle with the crumble topping. Bake at 375 F for 35 minutes. If it looks like the top of the pie is getting too browned, cover with an aluminum foil or lid for the last 10 minutes.

Let the apple pie cool. Then slice and serve.

Note: The flours in the crust can be replaced by the flour mix no. 2 (see page 276) or use your favorite gluten free flour mix. Video recipe also available on the blog.

Serving size: 1 slice: Calories: 335.6; Total Fat: 31.9 g; Total carbohydrate: 55.2 g; Protein: 4.4 g; Sugars: 28.9 g; Fiber: 5.7 g; Vitamin C: 1.3 %; Iron: 1.3 %; Calcium: 29 %.

Chocolate & Peanut Butter Bliss Balls

A healthy no-bake dessert or snack - a mix of granola bar and cookie dough. Great to curb the afternoon hunger and the dreaded mid afternoon energy slump. Loaded with protein, fiber and healthy fats to keep you full and satisfied whenever you a have a sweet craving.

Course: Dessert   Makes 17 balls   Ready in 20 min   GF, DF, V, P, W30

INGREDIENTS

5 medjool dates (pitted)
4 tbsp peanut butter (or almond butter)
1/3 cup almonds
1/3 cup walnuts
1/4 cup dairy-free mini chocolate chips
2 tbsp chia seeds (or use flax or hemp seeds)
1/3 cup gluten free rolled oats
2 tbsp maple syrup (optional)
1/2 coconut shreds
Pinch of salt

DIRECTIONS

1. Soak the dates in hot water for 10 min. Remove the pits and coarsely chop them. In your food processor, process the almonds, walnuts, dates, chia seeds and rolled oats until everything is finely chopped.

2. Add the rest of ingredients and process until the mixture is sticky enough to clump together or until it starts to form a ball.

If it seems too dry and isn't holding together, add a little peanut butter; if it's too sticky, add a few more oats.

3. Form little balls out of your mixture. You can also spoon out the mixture into mini silicon molds then refrigerate until they harden.

4. Once they are all rolled into balls, roll them in shredded coconut. This step just makes the balls have a more polished look to them plus they will not stick to each other.

5. Refrigerate for 1 hour, to allow them to set and flavors to meld. Store leftovers in an airtight container in the fridge. Remove from fridge 10 minutes before serving.

Notes And Suggestions

Leftovers can be refrigerated for up to 1 week.

Freeze for up to 3 months. Let thaw in the refrigerator overnight.

Serving size: 1 bliss ball: Calories: 121.9; Total Fat: 7.5 g; Total carbohydrate: 13.1 g; Protein: 3.1 g; Sugars: 7.5 g; Dietary Fiber: 2.4g; Vitamin E: 3.9 %; Vitamin A: 0.2%; Vitamin C: 0 %; Iron: 3.8 %; Calcium: 2.6 %.

Classic Carrot Cake With Coconut Frosting

The best, classic, soft and moist gluten free carrot cake made with pineapple, raisins and nuts arranged in three layers and finished with a dairy free coconut frosting. Great for Easter, birthdays an other celebrations.

Course: Dessert   Serves 8 people   Ready in 1h 30 minutes   GF, DF

INGREDIENTS

Cake batter:

2 large eggs
3/4 cup avocado oil
1 tsp vanilla extract
3/4 cup maple sugar
1 ½ cups lightweight flour blend (see page 272)
1 ½ tsp baking soda
1 tsp cinnamon powder
1/4 tsp nutmeg powder
1/2 tsp cardamom powder
1 ½ cups shredded carrots
1/4 cup walnuts, chopped
3/4 cup pineapple finely chopped
1/2 cup raisins or cranberries (dried)
1/4 tsp sea salt

Frosting:

coconut cream (without the water, aprox. 1 cup)
4 oz vegan butter
3/4 cup maple sugar
1 tsp vanilla extract
1/4 cup plant milk
Additional chopped walnuts to garnish

DIRECTIONS

1. Preheat oven to 360 F. Line a 9x13 inch rectangular baking pan with parchment paper and set aside.

2. In a large bowl, whisk together the sugar and eggs until combined and fluffy. Whisk in the oil, vanilla, pineapple followed by the dry ingredients until a cohesive batter comes together. Fold in the walnuts (or pecans), carrots, and raisins (if using) until combined.

3. Spread the batter evenly in the prepared pan and bake for approximately 30-35 minutes or until a toothpick inserted in the center comes out clean. Set aside to cool. Once cooled cut it in 3 equal parts. You will form a 3 layer cake (size: 8x4 inch).

4. In a bowl, cream together with an immersion mixer or a blender the coconut cream (room temp), the vegan butter (room temp), the plant milk, maple sugar and vanilla until smooth. The mixture will look runny first but if you place it in the fridge for at least 2 hours it will become hard enough to spread.

5. Spread the frosting evenly over each cake layer and finish by sprinkling with chopped walnuts or pecans, if using.

Notes And Suggestions

Store in the fridge for up to 4 days, or freeze for up to 2 months. Recipe can easily be doubled to make a larger cake.

Serving size: 1 slice: Calories: 536.7; Total Fat: 38.6 g; Total carbohydrate: 38.6 g; Protein: 8.7 g; Sugars: 23 g; Dietary Fiber: 2.5 g; Vitamin A: 40.5 %; Vitamin C: 7.9 %; Iron: 5.6%; Calcium: 2.7 %.

187

Fruit Tarts With Vanilla Pastry Cream

Gluten free shortcrust pastry filled with dairy free vanilla pastry cream, topped with fresh fruit and finished with a drizzle of chocolate.

Course: Dessert   Yields 12-13 fruit tarts   Ready in 1 h and 30 min   GF, DF

INGREDIENTS

The shortcrust:

1/2 cup (8 tbsp vegan butter, room temperature
1/3 cup maple sugar
1/2 tbsp vanilla extract
2 large eggs
1 ⅓ cup lightweight flour blend (see page 272)
1/8 teaspoon salt
add 1-2 tbsp cold water (if it's too thick)

The pastry cream:

1 ½ cups plant milk
6 tbsp maple sugar (or other granulated sweetener)
4 egg yolks
3 tbsp arrowroot powder
3 tbsp vegan butter
1 tsp vanilla extract
pinch of salt

Chcocolate drizzle

2 oz semisweet dairy free chocolate chips (melted)

Fruit: strawberries, blueberries

DIRECTIONS

1. Make the pastry cream in advance. In a saucepan, warm the milk over low heat until it is just hot enough to steam. While the milk is warming, whisk together the egg yolks, sugar, arrowroot powder, salt and vanilla until the mixture is thick and smooth. Remove the milk from heat. Slowly pour half, in a thin stream, into the egg mix, while whisking constantly. Then add the egg mix back into the hot milk. Heat it, over medium heat, whisking, until it starts to thicken (about 1-2 minutes). Remove from heat, stir in the vegan butter, and chill, then place in the fridge.

2. To make the crust: in a food processor add all ingredients, and process until dough just starts to come together to form a ball. If the dough is still crumbly, add 1 tbsp of cold water and mix again until it forms a slightly sticky ball of dough. Transfer to the fridge and chill for 20 minutes. When ready to bake the tartlets, preheat oven to 350 F. On a floured surface, or on an oily surface, roll out the dough to 1/8 inch thickness. Use a 5-inch diameter round lid and cut out 12 rounds of dough, gathering scraps and re-rolling as necessary. Place a round of dough into each ramekin. I used 3 inch wide ceramic round ramekins. Using your fingers, fit the dough on the walls (1 inch high because it will shrink a bit after baking).

Place each ramekin that is ready in the fridge to chill while you finish all of them. Prick the dough (bottom) a couple of times with a fork. Bake for 20-25 minutes, or until lightly browned. The shells will come out easily without greasing the ramekins. Allow to cool completely on baking rack.

3. Assemble the tarts. Spoon pastry cream into the tart shells. Melt the chocolate, place in a zip lock bag, cut a corner and drizzle over. Top with fresh fruits.

Keep refrigerated, covered for up to 2-3 days, then the tarts will start to get soggy. Do not freeze assembled tarts, only the crust can be frozen.

Serving size: 1 filled tart (no fruit): Calories: 213.3; Total Fat: 12.4 g; Total carbohydrate: 19.5 g; Protein: 3.2 g; Sugars: 8.5 g; Dietary Fiber: 0.9 g; Vitamin A: 3.9 %; Vitamin C: 3.7 %; Iron: 23.9 %; Calcium: 6.8 %.

Sour Cherry Coffee Cake

Easy delicious sour cherry cake with a light fluffy texture, no frosting and no decoration needed. Perfect for a cup of tea in the morning or as dessert after dinner.

Course: Dessert   Makes 8 slices   Ready in 45 min   GF, DF

INGREDIENTS

4 large eggs
3/4 cup maple sugar or other granulated sweetener
1 ½ cup lightweight flour blend (see page 272)
1/2 cup vegan butter, melted
2 cups sour cherries, pitted
1 tsp baking soda
1 tsp lemon juice
1/4 tsp salt
1 tsp vanilla extract
2 oz freeze dried fruit, powdered in a blender. Or use regular powdered sugar

DIRECTIONS

1. Preheat the oven to 350 F. Line with parchment paper the bottom of a round 10" springform pan.

2. Beat the eggs and sugar with a mixer until fluffy and foamy (7-8 minutes). Gently fold in the melted butter (not hot), the lemon juice and vanilla extract, stir just enough to combine.

3. Add the flour, salt and baking soda, and slowly mix to combine, so you keep the fluffiness intact. The final batter should be light and fluffy, a bit runny.

4. Spread half the batter into the prepared pan and sprinkle half of the cherries evenly, then pour over the other half of the batter and finish with another layer of sour cherries.

5. Bake for about 35 minutes. Check with a toothpick in the center, it should come out clean, and the top of the cake should be golden brown. Let the cake cool in the pan on a rack for 10 min. Then place it on a serving platter. Before serving, sprinkle it with powdered frozen fruit like pineapple or mango (to replace the regular sugar powder).

Notes And Suggestions

The cake is best for the first two days at room temperature. But it will keep for a few more days in the refrigerator.

Feel free to replace the flour mix with your favorite.

If you don't have fresh sour cherries use Dark Morello Pitted Sour Cherries in jar. They are available at Trader Joe's or Whole Foods.

Serving size: 1 slice: Calories: 258.6; Total Fat: 9.6 g; Total carbohydrate: 41.9 g; Protein: 4.9; Sugars: 19.3 g; Dietary Fiber: 2.3 g; Vitamin A: 12.7 %; Vitamin C: 3.1 %; Iron: 9.2 %; Calcium: 3.5 %; Vitamin E: 10.7%.

Apple Cinnamon Coffee Cake

A delicious, lightly sweet and moist apple cake flavored with cinnamon and topped with a generous layer of crunchy caramelized almonds. Serve for dessert with a cup of hot tea.

Course: Dessert   Makes 10 slices   Ready in 55 min   GF, DF, P

INGREDIENTS

Apple mixture:

3 large apples, thinly sliced
1 tbsp lemon juice
1/4 cup maple sugar, or coconut sugar
1 tsp cinnamon powder

Cake batter:

2 large eggs
3/4 cup plant milk
3/4 cup maple sugar or other granulated sugar
2 ½ cup grain free flour mix (see page 278)
1/2 cup vegan butter, melted
3/4 tsp baking soda
3/4 tsp baking powder
1/4 tsp sea salt
1 tsp vanilla extract

Topping:

1/3 to 1/2 cup sliced almonds
1 tbsp maple syrup
1 tbsp melted vegan butter

DIRECTIONS

1. Preheat oven to 350 F. In a medium saucepan combine apples (aprox. 4 cups), sugar, cinnamon, lemon juice and 1-2 tablespoons of water. Heat on medium heat for 5-6 minutes until apples soften. Set aside to cool.

3. Line the bottom of a 9×12 inch pan with parchment paper.

4. In a bowl mix plant milk, the eggs and vanilla until combined. Now add the flour (sifted), baking powder, baking soda, salt, and maple sugar, stir a bit, and the last add the melted vegan butter. Mix until just combined.

5. Spread 1/2 of the cake batter on the bottom of the prepared pan. Top with the apple mixture, spreading carefully to cover the batter. Then cover with the remaining batter. It's alright if it doesn't cover the apples entirely.

6. In a small bowl mix the sliced almonds with melted butter and maple syrup, mix to coat them. Sprinkle on top of the cake. This will make the top nicely caramelized, sweet and crunchy.

7. Bake 40 minutes, or until the center of the cake is set.

Notes And Suggestions:

The cake is best for the first two days. But it will keep for a few more days in the refrigerator. Reheat before serving.

Feel free to replace the flour mix with your favorite.

If you don't have apples, use pears.

Serving size: 1 slice: Calories: 282.3; Total Fat: 18.7 g; Total carbohydrate: 32.3 g; Protein: 4.9; Sugars: 12.3 g; Dietary Fiber: 3.9 g; Vitamin A: 1.7 %; Vitamin C: 5.7 %; Iron: 3.9 %; Calcium: 7.5 %; Vitamin E: 10.4%; Magnesium: 6.7%.

Rich Mocha Cake

This is a chocolate and coffee flavored cake, with a creamy dairy free mocha frosting. It's a rich moist and allergy friendly (for those sensitive to chocolate) dessert or birthday cake without refined sugar.

Course: Dessert   Makes 8 slices   Ready in 1 h 20 min   GF, DF

INGREDIENTS

Double

↓ **Cake batter:**

2 1 ½ avocado, ripe

4 2 large eggs

4 2 tbsp ground flax seed

/ 1 tbsp vanilla extract

1⅓ 2/3 cup non dairy milk

8 4 tbsp maple sugar or coconut sugar

pinch of stevia extract powder

4 2 tbsp coconut oil or butter

1½ 3/4 cup tigernut flour (or almond flour)

1½ 3/4 cup buckwheat flour

3/4 cup carob powder (or cacao if not allergic to chocolate)

1¼ 1 tsp baking soda

2 1 tsp apple cider vinegar

½ 1/4 tsp sea salt

4 Baking Powder

Frosting (make in advance):

1 ½ cup cashews, soaked

1 tbsp decaf freeze dried instant coffee

1/2 cup maple syrup

3 tbsp plant milk

juice of ½ lemon

1 ½ can coconut cream, solid

pinch of salt

pinch of stevia extract powder (or other sweetener)

DIRECTIONS

In doubling use 9" pans

Preheat the oven to 350 F and line a 6 inch round baking dish with parchment paper (cover the bottom only).

1. Prepare the batter: in a blender place the eggs, avocado, plant milk, ground flax seeds (to moisten), vanilla extract, coconut oil or butter, maple sugar and stevia (to add more sweetness, or use more sugar). Blend until you get a creamy texture. Transfer to a bowl.

To the bowl add the other dry ingredients (sifted, to remove lumps). At the end add the apple cider vinegar or lemon juice to activate the baking soda. Whisk until smooth. You should get a somewhat thick and sticky texture. Transfer to the baking dish. Bake for 30 minutes at 350 F. Cool in pan for 5 minutes, then transfer to a cooling rack to cool completely. Cut into two layers before assembling.

2. For the frosting: mix all ingredients in a blender until smooth. Refrigerate overnight to harden.

3. Assemble the cake: place one layer of the cooled cake on a serving platter. Top generously with frosting and smooth out to the edges. Top with the other cake layer and place in refrigerator for 30 minutes to set. Add another coat of frosting when chilled (picture 1).

4. Decorate. Place remaining cream in piping bag with star tip and decorate as you wish. Sprinkle with some carob powder or cacao powder (picture 2). Refrigerate for a few hours to set before serving.

Notes And Suggestions:

To get a thick layer of frosting between layers, apply it once, refrigerate to set and apply another layer, refrigerate again. Then proceed with cake topping. For visual instructions see recipe video on the blog.

Serving size: 1 slice: Calories: 505.2; Total Fat: 24.7 g; Total carbohydrate: 58.5 g; Protein: 16; Sugars: 31.5 g; Dietary Fiber: 7.5 g; Vitamin A: 2.5 %; Vitamin C: 8.7 %; Iron: 14.9 % ; Calcium: 3.5 %; Zinc: 8.5 %; Magnesium: 3.7%.

Cinnamon Maple Sugar Cookies

Cut out sugar cookies with cinnamon, walnut and maple flavor. The cookies are crisp, crumbly and addictive. No eggs, no dairy, no processed ingredients, just healthy vegan maple sugar cookies perfect for any holiday!

Course: Dessert   Makes 20 cookies   Ready in 1 hour   GF, DF, V

INGREDIENTS

Cookie batter:

1/2 cup walnut flour (grind in a blender)
1 cup sorghum flour
1/3 cup arrowroot flour
1/3 cup maple sugar
2 tbsp apple sauce
2 tbsp ground flax seed (golden)
1/2 cup vegan butter - Miyoko's
1/4 tsp sea salt
1/3 tsp baking powder
1/3 tsp ground vanilla bean, or extract

Cinnamon and maple sugar dusting:

1 ½ tbsp maple sugar
1 tsp cinnamon powder

DIRECTIONS

1. Prepare the ingredients. Place the cubed vegan butter in the freezer for 10-20 minutes before starting. And blend the walnuts into flour, use a coffee grinder or a blender.

2. Form the cookie dough. In a food processor, add the cold butter, the flours, the ground walnuts, maple sugar, salt, baking powder and ground vanilla bean (or vanilla extract). Pulse a few times until small crumbles form.

Then mix the apple sauce with ground flax seeds and add that to the food processor as well. Mix until the dough start to come together into larger crumbles.

The dough shouldn't be too thick or too sticky, just enough to form a soft pliable mass. Adjust by adding more flour or liquid if it doesn't feel right.

Gather the dough into a ball, wrap it and chill in the fridge for at least 30 minutes. This will help with an easier cutting.

Roll the dough out between two parchment papers until it is approx. 1/4 inch thick. Use cookie cutters and cut as many shapes as possible, re-rolling the dough scraps and cutting again.

Place the shapes on a baking sheet covered with parchment paper. Place in the freezer the cut cookies for another 10 minutes while the oven is pre-heating to 350 F.

3. Prepare the cinnamon and maple sugar dusting. In a coffee grinder combine 1.5 tbsp maple sugar and 1 tsp cinnamon, blend until you get a fine sugary powder.

Just before baking, take the cookies out from the fridge and dust the cinnamon and maple sugar powder all over them (use a sifter). The heat of the cookie will hold and melt the powder on the cookie so it won't fall off after baking. Another option is to dust them after baking, as soon as they come out of the oven.

4. Bake the cookies for 15 minutes. If you want browned crispier cookies - 20 minutes. Allow the cookies to cool for 2-3 minutes, then transfer them to a flat surface to cool. Once the cookies are cooled, they will get crispier.

Serving size: 1 cookie: Calories: 73; Total Fat: 4 g; Total carbohydrate: 9 g; Protein: 1.3; Sugars: 1.7 g; Dietary Fiber: 1.5 g; Vitamin A: 0 %; Vitamin C: 0.1 %; Calcium: 0.8 %; Iron: 2.9 %; Zinc: 0.5 %; Magnesium: 0.2 %.

Simple Vanilla Cake

A white vanilla cake with hints of almond and vanilla. The layers are moist, light, tender and coated in whipped white chocolate ganache. Feel free to substitute your favorite ingredients and lend your own touch to this cake.

Course: Dessert   Makes 8 slices   Ready in 5 hours   GF, DF

INGREDIENTS

Cake batter:

6 egg whites (medium eggs)
3/4 cup non dairy milk (the fatter the better)
2 ½ cups lightweight flour mix (see page 272)
1/3 cup almond flour (extra fine)
3/4 cup vegan butter
1 ½ cup maple sugar (or white sugar for a lighter color)
if you want it sweeter - add a pinch of stevia extract powder
2 tbsp vanilla extract
1 tsp baking soda
1 tsp baking powder
1/2 tsp lemon juice
1/2 tsp sea salt

Frosting (make at least 4 hours in advance):

11 ounces (310g) cacao butter (or use dairy free white chocolate)
13 ½ oz coconut whipping cream
1/3 cup + 1 tbsp vegan butter
1 tbsp vanilla extract
1/2 cup powdered sugar or use stevia extract powder (to preserve the white color; if you don't mind the color use powdered maple sugar)

DIRECTIONS

1. Prepare the ganache: In a sauce pan pour the coconut whipping cream, bring to almost a boil (turn off the heat) then add the cacao butter (or the white chocolate chips) and the vegan butter. Whisk the mixture until smooth and everything is melted. Refrigerate for at least 4 hours or overnight.

Preheat the oven to 350F and line two 9½-inch round cake pans with parchment paper (bottoms only).

2. Prepare the batter: whisk together the egg whites and the milk until slightly combined. Se aside.

In another bowl beat butter, sugar and vanilla extract for 2 minutes on medium speed, or until the sugar dissolves.

Add in the other dry ingredients (sifted, to remove lumps), except almond flour, mix until combined. Beat in the egg white mixture until is starts to fluff. At the end add the lemon juice and the almond flour, mix just to incorporate, don't overdo it. You should get a somewhat slightly thick and fluffy texture. Transfer to the pans (picture 1). Tap a few times to set. Bake for 25 minutes at 350 F. Cool in pan for 5 minutes, then transfer to a cooling rack to cool completely.

3. Assemble the cake: When ready to assemble, take out the ganache from the fridge, add the powdered sugar and vanilla and beat with an electric mixer until stiff peaks form (just like whipped cream). Place one layer of the cooled cake on serving platter, spread with half of ganache. Top with the other cake layer and spread the remaining ganache covering the top and sides of cake (picture 2).

4. Decorate with fresh berries and a sprinkle of grated chocolate. Refrigerate for a few hours to set before serving.

Notes And Suggestions:

If allergic to nuts, tigernut flour is a good substitute for the almond flour, or just use more of the flour mix.

Serving size: 1 slice: Calories: 659.2; Total Fat: 42.5 g; Total carbohydrate: 58.5 g; Protein: 12.1; Sugars: 20.4 g; Dietary Fiber: 3.5 g; Vitamin A: 0 %; Vitamin C: 0.2 %; Iron: 4.9 %; Calcium: 6.2 %; Zinc: 6.9 %; Magnesium: 11.7%.

Beverages (Hot & Cold)

Healthy drinks to enjoy during cold days or hot summer days, full of antioxidants and nutrients. All smoothies are made with a healthy blend of plant protein, fat and only natural sugar so you could enjoy them for breakfast and still get the necessary nutrition for the day. No added protein powders or processed food. All suitable for whole30 diet as well.

Tigernut & Coconut Milk

A nutrient dense and rich non-dairy milk alternative that you can make without using grains or nuts. It has a slightly sweet, nutty mellow flavor and is creamy due to coconut. The best tasting dairy free milk blend that uses only whole ingredients.

Course: Beverage   Makes 5 cups   Ready in 10 min   GF, DF, V, P, W30

INGREDIENTS

1 cup whole tigernuts, soaked
4 ½ cups warm filtered water
1/2 cup coconut cream
1 tsp vanilla extract
1 date, pitted, no skin
pinch Celtic sea salt

DIRECTIONS

1. Place the tigernuts in a bowl and pour boiled water to cover them, and soak at room temperature for 12-16 hours.

2. Discard the water, add soaked tigernuts, filtered warm water, coconut cream (from a can), vanilla extract, salt, and 1 date (pitted), preferably soft. Blend on high speed for about a minute, until the mixture looks creamy with small bits of tigernut pulp.

3. Strain the milk through the nutmilk bag into a container. Squeeze as much liquid as possible. Reserve the pulp for baking if you like.

Serve cold or warm, in drinks, smoothies, cereal bowls or porridge.

Notes And Suggestions

The boiling water will help "sterilize" the tigernuts and will keep the milk consumable longer. Also the hot water will help the tigernuts to soften faster. Make sure you use clean containers.

The milk will keep for 4-5 days in a airtight container in the fridge. Freeze in cubes for longer usage.

Serving size: 1 cup: Calories: 225; Total Fat: 11.2 g; Total carbohydrate: 32.2 g; Protein: 5.9 g; Sugars: 17.5 g; Dietary Fiber: 2 g; Iron: 0.1 %; Vitamin B-6: 0.1%; Magnesium: 0.4 %; Copper: 0.2 %.

Dairy Free Matcha Latte (Hot)

Rich aromatic matcha latte made with plant milk - an energizing alternative to coffee. Unlike coffee, caffeine in matcha takes longer to enter your system so it gives you the same energy without the sudden crash halfway through the day.

Course: Beverage   Makes 1 serving   Ready in 10 min   GF, DF, V, P, W30

INGREDIENTS

1 1/2 teaspoons matcha powder (ceremonial grade)
4 tablespoon hot water
1 ½ cups plant milk (I used tigernut and hemp milk)
2 dates (pitted)
1/2 tsp vanilla extract

If not whole30, to replace the dates, use 1 tsp maple sugar or maple cream

DIRECTIONS

1. In a large tall cup combine the hot water, dates (or maple sugar) and matcha. Blend with an immersion blender until the dates have totally broken down and the powder totally dissolved: about 1-2 minutes.

2. Meanwhile heat the milk on a low-medium flame in a small pot. When the milk is just coming to a simmer, mix it with the hand held mixer until it gets bubbly. Add vanilla. Pour over the matcha mixture. Serve!

Another option is to mix everything together in a blender if you don't prefer foamy layers.

Notes and Suggestions

Alternatively as a sweetener you can use honey or maple syrup (if not whole30). Or no sweetener at all.

Feel free to use any type of non-dairy milk you like.

Ceremonial grade matcha (and organic) is the best of the best; It has a more delicate, green tea flavor and is made from the youngest tea leaves, hence a higher quality. The culinary grade matcha is mostly used for baking and it has more bitter notes with a less vibrant color.

Serving size: 1 serving: Calories: 327; Total Fat: 10 g; Total carbohydrate: 60.3 g; Protein: 11 g; Sugars: 30.1 g; Dietary Fiber: 20 g; Vitamin A: 5%; Vitamin C: 7 %; Iron: 12 %; Calcium: 22.1 %; Vitamin D:10 %; Vitamin B-12: 10%; Magnesium: 11.6 %.

Hot Carob Cinnamon Drink

Sweet, nourishing, warm spiced carob milk with a slight earthy flavor. A hot milk beverage that is somewhat similar to hot chocolate but without cacao. This is a more healthier alternative to hot chocolate if you can't tolerate it.

Course: Beverage   Makes 1 serving   Ready in 7 min   GF, DF, V, P, W30

INGREDIENTS

1 ½ cups plant milk (I used a mix of coconut and tigernut)
2 tbsp carob powder (use cacao powder if not allergic to chocolate)
2 dates (or 2 tbsp maple syrup if not whole30)
1 tbsp maca powder
1/2 tsp vanilla extract
1/4 tsp cinnamon
Pinch of salt

DIRECTIONS

1. Pour the milk into a saucepan and heat over medium-low heat until hot, but not boiling.

2. Add the rest of ingredients and use your blender or your immersion blender to mix everything together until nice and smooth.

3. Pour into a cup or a mug, sit back, relax and enjoy!

Notes And Suggestions

Often seen as a cacao substitute, carob is not related to the cacao family at all and does not contain the caffeine or theobromine. The flavor although similar, has it's own unique flavor with caramel and earthy undertones, plus is high in antioxidants.

Compared to chocolate, carob is three times richer in calcium and it contains high amounts of fibre.

Maca is a powerful root from the Peruvian Andes with a sweet, malty taste. Maca is well known for its stamina and energy enhancing properties and is an excellent source of iron, magnesium, potassium, and iodine.

Serving size: 1 serving: Calories: 302.1; Total Fat: 6.5 g; Total carbohydrate: 60.5 g; Protein: 4.4 g; Sugars: 36.2 g; Dietary Fiber: 5.7 g; Vitamin A: 16.5%; Vitamin C: 4.4 %; Iron: 10.4 %; Calcium: 75.7 %; Vitamin B-12: 75%.

Mixed Berry Smoothie

A creamy low sugar mixed berry breakfast smoothie using plant based milk, yogurt and berries. Easy, quick and packed with plant based protein and fiber from hemp seeds and chia seeds. Make it the night before if you want to eat it with a spoon.

Course: Beverage   Makes 16 oz   Ready in 5 min   GF, DF, V, P, W30

INGREDIENTS

1/2 cups plant milk
1/2 cup plant based yogurt (plain)
1/2 cup raspberries
1/2 cup blueberries
1/2 cup blackberries
1/2 cup strawberries
1 tbsp chia seeds
1 tbsp hemp seeds

DIRECTIONS

1. Blend all ingredients until smooth. Either serve straight away or store in a clean and well covered container for up to a day.

Notes And Suggestions

If you want your smoothie thicker add ice or use frozen fruits. For more sweetness add a banana.

The hempseed's balance (3:1 ratio) of Omega-6 and Omega-3 linoleic acid is the perfect proportion for human dietary needs, making hemp an ideal protein and fiber addition to a healthy diet.

Hemp is also loaded with all 20 amino acids (including the nine essential) and taste similar to pine nuts.

Serving size: 8 oz: Calories: 303.8; Total Fat: 20.6 g; Total carbohydrate: 27.7 g; Protein: 6 g; Sugars: 10.8 g; Dietary Fiber: 13.3 g; Vitamin A: 2.9 %; Vitamin C: 69.2 %; Iron: 11.4 %; Calcium: 6.9 %; Magnesium: 21.3 %; Zinc: 7.2 %.

Tropical Green Smoothie

A refreshing mango pineapple smoothie with tropical flavors, packed with fiber, protein and bursting with Vitamin A and C. Sweet and delicious without added sugar. The best way to boost your nutrition and increase your serving of leafy green vegetables without resorting to salads.

Course: Beverage   Makes 16-18 oz   Ready in 7 min   GF, DF, V, P, W30

INGREDIENTS

1 cup coconut milk (or other plant based milk)
3/4 cup pineapple, cubed
1/2 medium mango, cubed
3 large kale leaves (Tuscan)
4-5 sprigs of parsley
1 tsp pumpkin seed butter (or 1 tbsp pumpkin seeds)

DIRECTIONS

1. Blend all ingredients in a high speed blender until completely smooth and creamy. Pour into a large glass and enjoy right away.

Notes And Suggestions

If you want your smoothie thicker add ice or use frozen fruits.

For more antioxidant and nutrients, you can add, 1 tsp of spirulina powder or matcha powder.

You can substitute any leafy green you like.

If you don't have plant milk, feel free to use a plain vegan yogurt or just water.

Try to drink it the same day (refrigarate if neccessary). The leafy greens degrade and loose nutrients faster than fruits when blended.

Raw pumpkin seeds provide a rich source of fiber, carbs and minerals. The seeds also boost your intake of protein - each ounce of seed provides almost 9 grams of protein.

Serving size: 18 oz: Calories: 277.2; Total Fat: 8.9 g; Total carbohydrate: 48.9 g; Protein: 6.9 g; Sugars: 30 g; Dietary Fiber: 6.5 g; Vitamin A: 351.7 %; Vitamin C: 291.2 %; Iron: 26.1 %; Calcium: 28.3 %, Vitamin B-12: 50.1 %; Vitamin D: 30%.

| Beverages (Hot & Cold)

Pink Summer Smoothie

A refreshing and tasty smoothie made with summer fruits. You will find this smoothie light and moderately sweet with fragrant notes of peach, mango and a minimal taste of cherry. The addition of mint makes it even more pleasant with a soothing effect to the stomach.

Course: Beverage   Makes 15-16 oz   Ready in 5 min   GF, DF, V, P, W30

INGREDIENTS

1 cup plant milk of your choice
2 small peaches, sliced
1/2 large mango, cubed
5-6 cherries (pitted)
1 tbsp chia seeds
5-6 fresh mint leaves

DIRECTIONS

1. Blend all ingredients in a high speed blender until completely smooth and creamy. Pour into a large glass and enjoy right away.

Notes And Suggestions

If you want your smoothie thicker add ice or use half of ingredients - frozen fruits. To make it sweeter use ripe fruits.

For more satiation, you can add, 1 tsp of nut butter or seed butter.

If you don't have plant milk, use a plain vegan yogurt or just water.

Try to drink it the same day (refrigerate if necessary).

Serving size: 8 oz: Calories: 174; Total Fat: 7.4 g; Total carbohydrate: 25.4 g; Protein: 5 g; Sugars: 16.5 g; Dietary Fiber: 6.9 g; Vitamin A: 16.3 %; Vitamin C: 33.9 %; Iron: 4.3 %; Calcium: 5.2 %; Magnesium: 8%; Zinc: 1 %.

Morning Mocha Smoothie

A rich filling smoothie with coffee and chocolate flavors: a fun way to switch up your morning cup of coffee or take it as an on-the-go breakfast. It's sweet and chocolatey and satisfying.

Course: Beverage   Makes 20 oz   Ready in 10 min   GF, DF, V

INGREDIENTS

2/3 cup cold coffee
1/2 cup plant milk of your choice
1 large ripe banana
1/2 cup cooked oatmeal
1 tsp raw cacao powder
1 tsp cashew butter (or any nut butter
2 medjool dates, pitted (soak in hot water for 15 minutes if they are not soft)

DIRECTIONS

1. Blend all ingredients in a high speed blender until completely smooth and creamy. Pour into a large glass and enjoy right away.

Notes And Suggestions

Cocoa or cacao, what's the difference? Raw cacao powder is made by cold-pressing unroasted cocoa beans, this process retains the living enzymes and removes the fat.

On the other hand, cocoa powder is the 'raw cacao' that's been roasted at high temperatures. The effect of roasting is lowering the overall nutritional value and destroying the health benefits. Usually raw cacao products are minimally processed, contain no added sugar and are higher in antioxidants.

If you want the smoothie thicker, add ice or use frozen fruit.

Use decaf coffee if you're worried about caffeine.

If you don't have plant milk, use a plain vegan yogurt or just water.

You can also use raw, soaked rolled oats but I find them harsher for my stomach than the cooked oats.

Serving size: 10 oz: Calories: 230.2; Total Fat: 5.3 g; Total carbohydrate: 43.9 g; Protein: 4.9 g; Sugars: 23.3 g; Dietary Fiber: 6.1 g; Vitamin A: 1.1 %; Vitamin B-6: 20.1 %; Vitamin C: 10.3 %; Iron: 5.6 %; Calcium: 1.7 %; Magnesium: 9.6 %; Zinc: 2 %.

Creamy Antioxidant-Rich Smoothie

A creamy tasty smoothie packed with plant based protein, antioxidants and vitamins with anti-inflammatory properties. The best part: you will not taste the greens at all.

Course: Beverage   Makes 25 oz   Ready in 5 min   GF, DF, V, P, W30

INGREDIENTS

1 ½ cup plant milk of your choice
1 large banana
10-12 medium strawberries
1/2 cup blueberries
1-2 cups of leafy greens (tightly packed)
1 tsp hemp seed butter (or 2 tbsp hemp seeds)

DIRECTIONS

1. Blend all ingredients in a high speed blender until completely smooth and creamy. Pour into a large glass and enjoy right away.

Notes And Suggestions

To make it sweeter use ripe fruits or add a sweetener of your choice.

The greens you can use: collard greens, parsley, spinach, kale, dandelions, swiss chard, beet greens or microgreens.

If you don't have plant milk, use a plain vegan yogurt or just water.

Try to drink it the same day (refrigerate if necessary).

Serving size: 12.5 oz: Calories: 204.3; Total Fat: 7.8 g; Total carbohydrate: 30.4 g; Protein: 7 g; Sugars: 16.5 g; Dietary Fiber: 7.2 g; Vitamin A: 114.4 %; Vitamin B-6:25.8 %; Vitamin C: 115.7 %; Iron: 16.9 %; Calcium: 6.3 %; Magnesium: 34.8%; Zinc: 12.6 %.

| Beverages (Hot & Cold)

Sunshine Burst Smoothie

Fresh carrot, orange blended with mango, and just a hint of ginger. It's full of vitamin A and C and makes a perfect post workout snack or light breakfast.

Course: Beverage   Makes 16 oz   Ready in 5 min   GF, DF, V, P, W30

INGREDIENTS

1 large orange, peeled, sliced and without pith
1 medium mango, peeled and cubed
1 large carrot, cubed
1/2 cup plant yogurt like cashew or coconut
1 inch fresh ginger, optional

DIRECTIONS

1. Blend all ingredients in a high speed blender until completely smooth and creamy. Pour into a large glass or two 8 oz glasses and enjoy right away.

Notes And Suggestions

To make it sweeter use ripe fruits or add a sweetener of your choice.

If you don't have plant yogurt use plant milk or just water.

To make it thicker use half of ingredients - frozen.

Serving size: 8 oz: Calories: 289.3; Total Fat: 12.1 g; Total carbohydrate: 39.4 g; Protein: 3.2 g; Sugars: 29.2 g; Dietary Fiber: 7.4 g; Vitamin A: 109.4 %; Vitamin B-6:13.5 %; Vitamin C: 142.4 %; Iron: 2 %; Calcium: 6.1 %; Magnesium: 6.3 %; Zinc: 1.4 %.

| Beverages (Hot & Cold)

Dressings And Sauces

This chapter includes healthy salad dressings, sauces and dips made with wholesome fresh ingredients or minimally processed. They are all dairy free, paleo and some whole30 friendly. They go well with raw salads, steamed veggies, as topping for baked root vegetables, cooked grains, or as dips with crudités.

Balsamic Vinaigrette With Herbs

This homemade balsamic vinaigrette has the perfect balance of tang, sweetness, vinegar and oil. It can be served over salads, steamed vegetables, pasta, used as a dipping sauce or a marinade for meat.

Course: Dressings   Makes 1 serving   Ready in 10 min   GF, DF, V, P, W30

INGREDIENTS

2/3 cup avocado oil or olive oil
1/3 cup balsamic vinegar
2 pitted dates
(or 1 tbsp maple syrup if not whole30)
1 tsp stone ground brown mustard
1/2 tsp sea salt
1/2 tsp black pepper
1 tsp minced fresh garlic
1 tsp minced red onion
1 tsp dried basil leaves
1 tsp dried parsley leaves

DIRECTIONS

1. Combine all ingredients in a small jar or a blender (or immersion blender) and mix until the ingredients are combined and smooth.

2. Taste. Then add more salt or vinegar if you prefer it more tangy.

3. Let the dressing stand 10 minutes for the flavors to blend, then serve or refrigerate for up to 2 weeks.

Notes And Suggestions

Dressing will thicken as it chills, so stir in 1-2 tbsp of water to thin it out. The recipe below makes aprox. 1 cup, but you can use the proportions to make any amount.

This recipe also works great with any kind of vinegar you like, including red wine vinegar or apple cider vinegar, but balsamic is the most aromatic.

Check the label if you are allergic to sulfites. Not all balsamic vinegars have sulfites, but many less expensive choices do.

Serving size: **1/4 cup:** Calories: 369; Total Fat: 37.3 g; Total carbohydrate: 12.3 g; Protein: 0.4 g; Sugars: 7.4 g; Dietary Fiber: 0.9 g; Vitamin A: 0.7%; Vitamin C: 1.1 %; Iron: 1.6 %; Calcium: 1 %.

| Dressings And Sauces

Creamy Raspberry Vinaigrette

A smooth and creamy raspberry vinaigrette dressing that goes well with any green salad. The taste is out of this world good! You can make it with fresh raspberries, frozen or freeze dried raspberries.

Course: Dressings   Makes 1 cup   Ready in 10 minutes   GF, DF, V, P, W30

INGREDIENTS

1/2 cup plant yogurt – coconut or cashew works well
2 tbsp avocado oil
3 tbsp lemon juice or apple cider vinegar
1/2 cup frozen or fresh raspberries
2 tsp Dijon mustard
2 medium garlic cloves, fresh
1 tsp onion powder
2 tsp maple syrup (omit if whole30, replace with 2 dates)
pink salt (about 1/2 tsp) and pepper - to taste

DIRECTIONS

1. Combine all ingredients in a jar and blend with an immersion blender until combined and smooth.

2. Taste and add more salt if necessary.

3. Let the the flavors to meld for at least 30 minutes, then serve. Or refrigerate for up to 10 days if you used fresh raspberries, and up to two weeks, when you use freeze dried raspberries.

Notes And Suggestions

In order to get a more concentrated flavor I also like to use freeze dried raspberries, it makes such a huge difference! Add additional 2 tsp freeze dried raspberries (powdered).

If you're using homemade coconut yogurt without additives, make sure to add it at the end or it will curdle while blending.

Serving size: 1/4 cup: Calories: 161.9; Total Fat: 14.5 g; Total carbohydrate: 7.5 g; Protein: 1 g; Sugars: 3.4 g; Dietary Fiber: 2.7 g; Vitamin A: 0.6%; Vitamin C: 8.6 %; Iron: 1 %; Calcium: 1 %; Magnesium: 1.7 %; Zinc: 1.5 %.

Ranch Dressing

A super flavorful vegan, oil free ranch dressing made from scratch with real whole ingredients. It's healthier (no additives, preservatives and gums), more budget-friendly, and easy to make!

Course: Dressings **Makes 1 cup** **Ready in 10 minutes** GF, DF, V, P, W30

INGREDIENTS

1/2 cup coconut yogurt (or other plain plant yogurt, also you can use coconut kefir or vegan mayo)
3 tbsp coconut cream
1 tbsp lemon juice or apple cider vinegar
1/2 tsp brown mustard or Dijon mustard
1 large garlic clove, fresh
2 green onions (the white part only)
1 tsp dried parsley (or 1 tbsp freshly chopped)
1 tsp dried dill weed (or 1 tbsp fresh, chopped)
1/2 tsp Celtic sea salt
dash of black pepper

DIRECTIONS

1. Chill a can of coconut milk for at least 1 hour in advance, turn it upside down and open the can. Pour the water in a separate container then scoop the cream in the jar you will use for mixing.

2. Add in the plant yogurt, lemon juice, garlic, onion, mustard, salt, and black pepper. Use an immersion blender to mix until smooth. Then add dill and parsley give it a stir and refrigerate the dressing for at least 30 minutes to let the flavors meld together. The dressing will thicken up as it sits in the fridge.

Notes And Suggestions

Add the herbs at the end so you don't turn the whole dressing green. For a cheesy flavor add 1 tsp nutritional yeast as well.

You can use a mix of fresh herbs and dry herbs for best flavor. To keep the dressing longer (up to 10 days), use dried herbs only. With fresh herbs the dressing is good only for 3-4 days.

Some prefer to add 1-2 tbsp mayonnaise (vegan or not). Just make sure you use high quality, whole30 and paleo approved, like Tessemae's.

To avoid curdling, add the yogurt at the end and don't overmix. Curdling usually happens when you use homemade (coconut) yogurt because it doesn't contain thickening agents and gums.

Serving size: 1/4 cup: Calories: 93.9; Total Fat: 7.3 g; Total carbohydrate: 5.2 g; Protein: 2.3 g; Sugars: 3 g; Dietary Fiber: 1.2 g; Vitamin A: 3.1 %; Vitamin B-6: 0.7 %; Vitamin C: 7.1 %; Iron: 1.1 %; Calcium: 1 %; Magnesium: 0.7 %.

Creamy Avocado Dressing

This creamy flavorful avocado dressing is packet with healthy fats and will increase the nutrient absorption from all the veggies and greens. It can be served over salads, steamed vegetables, used for bowl meals or as a dipping sauce.

Course: Dressings   Makes 1 ½ cups   Ready in 10 min   GF, DF, V, P, W30

INGREDIENTS

1 large ripe avocado
1/3 cup plant milk
2 tbsp lemon juice
2 fresh garlic cloves
1 tsp stone ground brown mustard
1 ½ tsp onion powder (or 2 tbsp freshly minced)
1 tsp dried basil
1 tsp Celtic sea salt
dash of black pepper
1 tbsp maple syrup or honey (optional) remove if you need it whole30 compliant

DIRECTIONS

1. In a mini food processor or in a immersion blender container add all the ingredients together.

2. Process or blend until smooth. Thin out the salad dressing with a bit more plant milk if you want a thinner consistency.

Notes And Suggestions

The dressing thickens up a bit as it sits in the fridge. The taste becomes much flavorful too, as the flavors meld together.

Keep in an airtight container for up to 5-6 days, but 3 to 4 days is best.

Serving size: 1/4 cup: Calories: 65.7; Total Fat: 5.1 g; Total carbohydrate: 5.1 g; Protein: 0.7 g; Sugars: 2.1 g; Dietary Fiber: 2 g; Vitamin A: 0.9 %; Vitamin C: 4.5 %; Iron: 1.5 %; Calcium: 0.7 %; Magnesium: 3.4 %.

Honey Mustard Sauce

This tangy, creamy, sweet sauce is good on everything: meat, salads, sandwiches and wraps. It stores well in the fridge, and if you want to make it whole30 compliant, replace the honey with soaked pitted dates.

Course: Dressings   Makes 3/4 cup   Ready in 5 min   GF, DF, P

INGREDIENTS

1/4 mayonnaise
1/4 cup organic raw honey
3 tbsp Dijon mustard
1 tbsp stone ground brown mustard
1/4 - 1/2 tsp turmeric powder (for color)
dash of black pepper

DIRECTIONS

1. Combine all the ingredients in a jar and stir until smooth. Store in the refrigerator in an airtight container for up to a week.

It's even better the next day, so make it ahead of time if you can.

Notes And Suggestions

Use good quality organic mayo (soy free, paleo and whole30 compliant) like Tessemae's or Chosen Foods.

Add some cayenne pepper if you prefer a little kick.

Because the mustard contains some acidity from apple cider vinegar there is not need to add any lemon juice.

Serving size: 2 tbsp: Calories: 110.2; Total Fat: 10.6 g; Total carbohydrate: 11.7 g; Protein: 0 g; Sugars: 10.7 g; Dietary Fiber: 0.1 g; Vitamin A: 0%; Vitamin C: 0.1 %; Iron: 0.3%; Calcium: 0 %; Magnesium: 0 %.

Refreshing Citrus Vinaigrette

A light healthy dressing for summer salads with a balanced tartness and sweetness. It has refreshing lemon and orange notes and healthy fats that will absorb all those fat soluble vitamins. It is also fabulous with grilled chicken, as well as fish and seafood.

Course: Dressings   Makes 1 cup   Ready in 10 min   GF, DF, V, P, W30

INGREDIENTS

1/4 cup oil (extra virgin olive oil, avocado oil or flaxseed oil)
1/3 cup fresh orange juice (half of large orange)
1/3 cup fresh lemon juice (1 large lemon)
2 tsp Dijon mustard
1 clove garlic
1 tbsp minced onion
1/2 tsp salt
1/6 tsp black pepper
1 tsp maple syrup, or honey (remove if whole30)
1 tbsp chopped fresh tarragon (optional)

DIRECTIONS

1. Juice lemon and orange. Mince garlic and onion.

2. Whisk or shake together all ingredients until well blended (it will separate with time). For a smoother consistency (a perfectly emulsified dressing) use an immersion blender and a tall narrow container and a few seconds.

3. Dip a green leaf into the dressing and taste. Adjust any of the seasonings if necessary.

4. Refrigerate for up to 10-14 days. Whisk or shake before each use.

Notes And Suggestions

Use good quality organic cold pressed oils for salads. As a healthier alternative you can use flaxseed oil with Omega-3 fatty acids. This oil should never be heated because it can easily oxidize and lose too many of its valuable nutrients, so it's perfect for salads!

Tarragon has a slightly bittersweet flavor and an aroma similar to anise. If you don't like it, use other herbs.

Serving size: 1/4 cups: Calories: 152.6; Total Fat: 14.1 g; Total carbohydrate: 5.4 g; Protein: 0.3 g; Sugars: 3.5 g; Dietary Fiber: 0.1 g; Vitamin A: 0.4 %; Vitamin C: 27.1 %; Iron: 0.5%; Calcium: 0.6 %.

Creamy Basil Pesto Sauce

This basil sauce is made of fresh basil leaves, garlic, nut and seed butters, olive oil and freshly squeezed lemon juice. Blended together these make a creamy green sauce that can be used basically on anything that needs some extra flavor.

Course: Dressings   Makes 8 oz   Ready in 10 min   GF, DF, V, P, W30

INGREDIENTS

2 cups fresh basil, packed
2 garlic cloves
1/4 of a small onion
2 tsp pumpkin seed butter (or use 3 tbsp pumpkin seeds)
2 tsp cashew butter (or use 2 tbsp cashews)
2 tbsp olive oil
1/2 tsp stone ground brown mustard
1/4 cup lemon juice (one lemon)
3/4 tsp Celtic sea salt
pinch of black pepper
1 tbsp maple syrup (omit if whole30)

DIRECTIONS

1. Combine all ingredients in a small food processor, blender or use hand held mixer and a tall container. Mix until you obtain a creamy mass.

2. Taste and adjust the seasonings to your liking.

Notes And Suggestions

Alternatively, experiment with other nut and seed butters: walnuts, pistachios, almonds, or sunflower seeds.

Any sort of greens can be used instead of the basil — like parsley, cilantro, mint, spinach or kale.

To make it thicker use less oil and more seeds / nuts. To make it thinner add a bit of water. To freeze, spoon it into ice cube trays.

Serve with gluten free pasta, rice, beans, use as pizza sauce, toss with your salad, spread on sandwiches, spoon over grilled meat or fish.

Serving size: 2 tbsp: Calories: 104.8; Total Fat: 5.8 g; Total carbohydrate: 14.4 g; Protein: 3.6 g; Sugars: 2.1 g; Dietary Fiber: 7.5 g; Vitamin A: 33.8 %; Vitamin B-6: 21.7 %; Vitamin C: 22.9 %; Iron: 44.5 %; Calcium: 39 %; Magnesium: 21.1 %; Zinc: 8.4 %.

Nut Free Chickpea Sauce

Chickpeas blended nicely into a creamy sauce flavored with herbs and spices and it doesn't require dairy or nuts of any sort. Use it as a base for a creamy soup, for dipping veggies, as burrito sauce or any other vegan dish.

Course: Dressings   Makes 12 oz   Ready in 10 min   GF, DF, V

INGREDIENTS

1 cup cooked chickpeas
1 cup chickpea water (from can)
1 ½ tbsp lemon juice
1 large garlic clove
1/2 tsp onion powder
2 tsp Dijon mustard
1/2 tsp dried dill weed
1/2 tsp dried basil leaves or 1 tbsp fresh basil, chopped
1/4 tsp dried oregano
1 tbsp maple syrup
1/2 tsp Celtic sea salt

DIRECTIONS

1. Combine all ingredients in a small food processor, blender or use hand held mixer and a tall container. Mix until you obtain a creamy mass.

2. Taste and adjust the seasonings to your liking.

Notes And Suggestions

Alternatively, experiment with other herbs and spices. Add nutritional yeast for a cheesy flavor.

If the garlic seems too strong for you, sauté it in a pan with a touch of olive oil until golden brown, then add it in the blender with the rest of ingredients.

Serve with gluten free pasta, rice, beans, toss with your salad, veggies, or spread on sandwiches and burritos.

Serving size: 2 tbsp: Calories: 29.3; Total Fat: 0.4 g; Total carbohydrate: 5.3 g; Protein: 1.3 g; Sugars: 1.8 g; Dietary Fiber: 1.1 g; Vitamin A: 0.2 %; Vitamin B-6: 0.3 %; Vitamin C: 2.6 %; Iron: 0.4 %; Calcium: 0.3 %; Magnesium: 0.5 %; Zinc: 0.5 %.

Wholesome BBQ Sauce

Thick, tangy, and sweet, with a hint of smoke and spice. Made from wholesome ingredients, this BBQ sauce recipe is made without refined sugar or other processed ingredients. Brush it onto veggies, your favorite piece of meat or use it as a dipping sauce.

Course: Dressings   Makes 2 ½ cup   Ready in 25 min   GF, DF, V, P, W30

INGREDIENTS

1 ½ cups diced tomatoes
1/2 cup tomato paste
2 tbsp olive oil
1 medium onion, fresh, diced
3-4 cloves of garlic, diced
1 tbsp stone ground brown mustard
1 stalk of celery, diced
1/3 cup apple cider vinegar
1/3 cup coconut aminos
1 tsp dried basil
1 tbsp smoked paprika
1/2 tsp red pepper flakes - or 1 tsp chili powder
1 tsp Himalayan pink salt
1/2 tsp black pepper
pinch of stevia extract powder (optional, to make it more sweet) or use some maple sugar

DIRECTIONS

1. Add oil to a saucepan and heat over medium heat. Add onion and garlic and sauté until fragrant, about 3-4 minutes.

2. Make sure to stir and watch the garlic, it can burn easily.

Add the rest of ingredients including the seasonings and spices. Stir to combine

3. Allow mixture to come to a simmer over medium-low heat and cook for about 2-3 minutes, stirring. Use a lid to prevent splashing.

4. Taste and adjust seasoning for desired flavor. Cool. Transfer to a tall jar (to prevent splashing) and use an immersion blender right in the jar to blend everything together until smooth. You can also use a regular high speed blender.

Notes And Suggestions

To make this BBQ sauce really spicy add ¼ tsp ground up chile peppers such as cayenne, chipotle, or add a few splashes of your favorite spicy hot sauce.

It stays fresh in the fridge for up to 2 weeks (in an airtight container).

Serving size: 2 tbsp: Calories: 25.2; Total Fat: 1.5 g; Total carbohydrate: 2.7 g; Protein: 0.4 g; Sugars: 1.7 g; Dietary Fiber: 0.6 g; Vitamin A: 3.6 %; Vitamin C: 5.7 %; Iron: 1.1 %; Calcium: 7 %; Magnesium: 0.7 %.

Creamy Cauliflower Sauce

A creamy rich sauce that can be used as Alfredo sauce, pizza sauce, pasta, as a dip or in casseroles. It can be seasoned and tailored to any vegan and gluten free recipe.

Course: Dressings   **Makes 4-5 cups**   **Ready 1 hour**   GF, DF, V, P, W30

INGREDIENTS

1 small head of cauliflower (use florets only)
2 garlic cloves
1/2 cup raw cashews (soaked)
1 ½ cup stock (vegetable or chicken)
1/2 cup plant milk
1/2 tbsp fresh lemon juice
1/3 tsp Celtic sea salt
1 tsp onion powder
1 tsp Dijon Mustard
2 tbsp vegan butter
2 tsp Coconut Aminos

DIRECTIONS

1. Soak cashews for at least 1 hour in hot water, drain.

2. Place the stock, cauliflower and garlic in a small pot and bring to a boil. Let it cool a bit, then transfer to a blender.

3. Add the rest of ingredients - mix until smooth and creamy.

Let it cool, then transfer to airtight container and refrigerate for up to 4-5 days.

Notes And Suggestions

It the sauce looks too thick for you, add more stock, make sure to taste before adding more salt.

Serve it over your roasted vegetables, or a bowl of pasta.

If you want a cheesy flavor add 2 tbsp nutritional yeast.

If you want a less pronounced garlic flavor, sauté it separately. Do not boil.

Serving size: 1 cup: Calories: 161.4; Total Fat: 13 g; Total carbohydrate: 7.4 g; Dietary Fiber: 2.7 g; Sugars: 2.5 g; Protein: 3.7 g; Vitamin A: 1.1 %; Vitamin B-12: 0 %; Vitamin B-6: 6 %; Vitamin C: 46.3 %; Calcium: 4.3 %; Iron: 5.7 %; Magnesium: 1.5 %.

Breads, Rolls, Tortillas

Naturally leavened breads (sourdough) and unleavened made with clean unprocessed ingredients, mostly wholegrain, with addition of fruits or vegetables.

Simple Gluten Free Tortillas

Make your meals portable with these gluten free tortillas. Make burritos, taquitos, quesadillas, tacos, wraps or roll-ups. They can be warmed in the oven, steamed, grilled, fried, toasted or baked in the oven to make tortilla chips.

Makes 5 tortillas   Ready in 35 minutes   GF, DF, V

INGREDIENTS

1 ½ cup lightweight flour blend (see page 272)
2 ½ tsp ground flax seeds
2 tsp psyllium husk
2 tbsp coconut cream (or vegan butter)
8 ½ tbsp warm water
1 tbsp lemon juice or apple cider vinegar
1/2 tsp Celtic sea salt

Optional:

1/2 tsp dried garlic powder
1/2 tsp dried onion powder

DIRECTIONS

1. In a food processor combine all ingredients and process until a soft dough forms. Just like a pie crust but slightly sticky. It's ok if the dough looks a bit moist. Form dough into a ball and let it rest wrapped for 10 minutes. The psyllium husk and flax seeds will absorb all the moisture.

2. Pre-heat your skillet on a medium heat (5-6) for about 5-10 minutes.

3. Cut the dough into 5 portions and shape into balls. Take one and the rest cover to prevent drying.

4. Place the ball dough between 2 plastic wraps and roll with a rolling pin as thin as possible. Or use a tortilla press if you have one. No additional flour needed.

5. Remove the top layer of plastic wrap and flip the tortilla gently over on your hand and remove the other plastic wrap, transfer directly in the skillet. Cook the tortilla approximately 30-45 seconds on each side. Do not overcook otherwise, you will end up with a very crisp/ fried tortilla.

Notes And Suggestions

If the dough looks too stiff, add a bit of more liquid.

Once cooked keep the tortillas moist and warm until you're all done cooking them – then transfer to a ziplock bag and keep them on the counter for up to 3-4 days.

Serving size: 1 Tortilla: Calories: 160.2; Total Fat: 1.8 g; Total carbohydrate: 32.2 g; Protein: 4.5 g; Sugars: 1.2 g; Dietary Fiber: 4.7 g; Iron: 2.6 %; Calcium: 1.2 %; Vitamin B-6: 5.8 %; Magnesium: 5.3 %.

Soft Potato Tortillas

These are very thin, soft, chewy and flexible tortillas made with leftover mashed potatoes. Make burritos, taquitos, quesadillas, tacos, wraps or roll-ups. They can be warmed, grilled, fried or baked in the oven to make tortilla chips.

Makes 5 (9") tortillas   Ready in 40 minutes   GF, DF, V

INGREDIENTS

Mashed potatoes (1 cup)

3 medium potatoes, steamed or boiled (no liquid) and mashed.
2 tbsp vegan butter
1 tbsp hot water (from steamer, to thin out)
3/4 tsp sea salt
dash black pepper
1/2 tsp onion powder
1/2 tsp garlic powder

Dough:

3/4 cup gluten free sourdough starter (see page 280)
2 tsp psyllium husk
2-3 tbsp arrowroot flour
1/2 tsp baking powder (optional, for puffier tortillas)
Video recipe available on the blog.

DIRECTIONS

1. Prepare the mashed potatoes. Place and cook the potatoes (cubed) in a steamer, for 15-20 minutes, until tender. Remove and mash with a fork; take out 1 cup and to that add 1 tbsp of hot water from steamer, the vegan butter and seasonings. Mix until smooth and set aside.

2. Form the Dough. In a separate bowl take the sourdough starter from the fridge, measure 3/4 cup and put the rest back. Mine is thicker than a pancake batter, if yours is thinner add a bit of more flour (the flour your sourdough is made of) to it, to thicken up. To that add psyllium husk and the potato mixture, mix well and let it rest covered for 15 minutes, to absorb the moisture.

3. When ready to cook, add the arrowroot starch (you might need less or more then specified) and baking powder - you will have a very soft dough - like a cookie dough (picture 1).

4. Pre-heat your skillet (I used non-stick ceramic) on medium heat (5-6) for 5-8 minutes.

5. Shape the dough and cook. Cut the dough and shape into 5 balls. Cover the rest while you work with the dough. Place the ball dough between 2 parchment papers and roll with a rolling pin as thin as possible (picture 2), the tinner the better.

6. Remove the top layer of paper and flip the tortilla gently over directly into the skillet. Then slowly remove the other paper (will detach easier if you wait 10-15 seconds; picture 3). Use a bit of oil if your skillet is not non-stick.

7. Cook the tortilla approximately 30-45 seconds on each side.

8. Once cooked keep the tortillas moist & warm (covered). Transfer to a ziplock bag and keep on the counter for up to 3-4 days. Or freeze for longer.

Serving size: 1 Tortilla: Calories: 146.6; Total Fat: 4.7 g; Total carbohydrate: 27.8 g; Protein: 2.5 g; Sugars: 0.6 g; Dietary Fiber: 3 g; Vitamin C: 5.3%; Iron: 3.5 %; Calcium: 3.9 %; Vitamin B-6: 12.9 %; Manganese: 50.3 %.

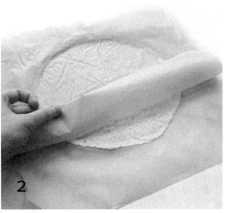

Sweet Potato Tortillas

These are very thin, soft, chewy, flexible and slightly sweet tortillas due to mashed sweet potatoes. They are great just by themselves, but also with savory or sweet fillings. Use them as a base for tacos, burritos, quesadillas, and nachos. Or make tortilla chips.

Makes 5 (9") tortillas   Ready in 40 minutes   GF, DF, V

INGREDIENTS

Mashed sweet potatoes (1 cup)

1 medium sweet potato, peeled, steamed or boiled (no liquid) and mashed.
2 tbsp vegan butter
3/4 tsp sea salt
1/2 tsp onion powder
1/2 tsp garlic powder

Dough:

3/4 cup gluten free sourdough starter (see page 280)
2 tsp psyllium husk
1/3 cup arrowroot flour
1/2 tsp baking powder (optional, for puffier tortillas)

DIRECTIONS

1. Prepare the mashed sweet potatoes. Place and cook the potatoes (cubed) in a steamer, for 15-20 minutes, until tender. Remove and mash with a fork; take out 1 cup and to that add the vegan butter and seasonings. Mix until smooth and set aside cool.

2. Form the dough. In a separate bowl take the sourdough starter from the fridge, measure 3/4 cup and put the rest back. Mine is thicker than a pancake batter, if yours is thinner add a bit more flour (the flour your sourdough is made of) to it, to thicken up.

To that add psyllium husk and the potato mixture, mix well and let it rest covered for 15 minutes, to absorb the moisture.

3. When ready to cook, add the arrowroot starch (you might need less or more then specified), and baking powder - you should have a very soft dough - like a sticky cookie dough (picture 1).

4. Pre-heat your skillet (I used non-stick ceramic) on medium heat (5-6) for 5-8 minutes.

5. Shape the dough and cook. Cut the dough and shape into 5 balls. Cover the rest while you work with the dough. Place the ball dough between 2 parchment papers and roll with a rolling pin as thin as possible (picture 2).

6. Remove the top layer of paper and flip the tortilla gently directly into the skillet. Then slowly remove the other paper (it will detach easier if you wait 10-15 seconds; picture 3).

7. Cook the tortilla approximately 30-45 seconds on each side.

8. Once cooked keep the tortillas moist & warm (covered). Transfer to a ziplock bag and keep on the counter for up to 3-4 days or freeze.

Serving size: 1 Tortilla: Calories: 179.6; Total Fat: 4.7 g; Total carbohydrate: 32 g; Protein: 2.4 g; Sugars: 1.6 g; Dietary Fiber: 3.3 g; Vitamin A: 27.4 %; Vitamin C: 5.6 %; Iron: 4.5 %; Calcium: 3 %; Vitamin B-6: 13.6 %.

| Breads Rolls Tortillas

Dark Whole Grain Bread

Easy gluten free sourdough bread that doesn't require kneading, shaping or Dutch oven. It has only healthy whole grain gluten free flours and seeds plus it's xanthan gum free, yeast free, egg free, dairy free and sugar free.

Makes 1 loaf (20 slices)   Ready in 6 hours   GF, DF, V

INGREDIENTS

1 ½ cup sourdough starter, active (see page 280)
3 ½ cups flour blend no. 1 (see page 274)
1/3 cup oil (or vegan butter, for a softer bread)
1 ½ tbsp psyllium husk
2 ½ cup of filtered water
2 tsp Celtic sea salt

Note:

As seen in the picture, for this bread baking I used a 18x7x3.5" clay pan, and another one (same size) as covering.
To produce a nice crunchy crust on all sides, heat the second pan for 10 minutes in the oven before placing on top. Giving bread the highest heat possible at the beginning will ensure that the trapped gasses can force the bread to increase in volume as quickly as possible.

DIRECTIONS

1. Form the dough. Once the starter is active (is bubbling regularly within a few hours of feeding) take the amount of starter you need (1 ½ cup). To that add the rest of ingredients: the flour (sifted), psyllium husk, water (or plant milk), the oil (or vegan butter) and salt.

Mix to combine. The dough should look like a thick brownie batter. No kneading is required. Prepare the baking pan by lining it with parchment paper (or at least the bottom), to prevent sticking. Scrape the dough into the pan and smooth it out with a spatula for a nice dome shape (picture 1). Sprinkle seeds or nuts if you want. Cover with a plastic wrap or a towel to seal moisture (you can also spray the inside of the wrap with water to prevent dough from cracking) and let it rise in a warm place approximately 4-5 hours (picture 2). It depends on how warm is your kitchen.

2. Bake the bread. Preheat oven at 425 degrees F. When ready to bake, remove the wrap, cover with another baking tin (same size), or a lid or with aluminum foil (without touching it). Make sure it's tight so the hot air is trapped inside and ensure a better rise. Turn the temperature down to 380 F (200 C) and bake for 30 minutes. Then bake uncovered for another 40-45 minutes until golden brown.

Allow to cool for 15-20 minutes before taking the bread out of the tin. And cool completely before handling or slicing (use a serrated knife). The slices can be stored in a closed container at room temperature for up 4-6 days. Freeze for longer storage. When needed, slices can go from freezer to toaster directly. Personally I like double toasting or toasting at the highest intensity of my toaster, the texture and smell is just like freshly baked bread!

Serving size: 1 slice: Calories: 157.5; Total Fat: 5.3 g; Total carbohydrate: 24.2 g; Protein: 3.4 g; Sugars: 0.1 g; Dietary Fiber: 3.5 g; Calcium: 1.8 %; Vitamin B-6: 6.3 %; Iron: 6.5 %; Magnesium: 5.6 %; Zinc: 2.8 %.

Pumpernickel Bread

It's dark, hearty, slightly tangy, but also slightly sweet and molasses-like. Kind of tastes like rye bread but without gluten, commercial yeast, baking powder, or xanthan gum. It's a satisfying accompaniment to soup or on a platter with dips, olives and crudites - as crackers.

Makes 1 loaf (20 slices)   Ready in 6 hours   GF, DF, V

INGREDIENTS

1 ½ cup sourdough starter, active (see page 280)
1 ½ cup buckwheat flour
2/3 cup teff flour
1/2 cup ground flax seeds
2 tbsp sunflower seeds (ground like flour)
2 tbsp pumpkin seeds (ground like flour)
2 tbsp caraway seeds, ground
1 tbsp coriander seeds, ground
2 tbsp psyllium husk
2 tbsp maple sugar, or coconut sugar
2 ½ tsp Celtic sea salt
2 ½ cups filtered water (+2 or 3 tbsp more if needed)
2 tbsp cacao powder (optional - for a more dark color) or use carob powder
Video recipe available on the blog.

DIRECTIONS

1. Form the dough. Proceed to this step when the starter is active (is bubbling regularly within a few hours of feeding). To the starter add the wet ingredients, whisk a bit and add the rest the flours (sifted), psyllium husk, the seeds (freshly milled in a blender and sifted, to avoid clumps and provide more air), sugar, cacao powder and salt. Mix to combine. The dough should look like a very thick (hard to mix) brownie batter. But be careful if it's too thick it will not rise much. If it's too thin it will not bake evenly in the middle, the texture will be more gummy.

Prepare the baking pan (I used a 9x5" glass pan) by lining it with parchment paper. Scrape the dough into the pan and smooth it out with a spatula for a nice dome shape. Sprinkle caraway seeds (picture 1). Cover with plastic wrap or a towel to seal moisture and let it rise in a warm place approximately 4-5 hours (picture 2). The time depends on how warm is your kitchen.

2. Bake the bread. Preheat oven at 425 degrees F. When ready to bake, remove the wrap, place another heavy bread pan on top that fits tightly (I usually heat it for 10 minutes in the oven first. Giving bread the highest heat possible at the beginning will ensure that the trapped gasses can force the bread to increase in volume as quickly as possible). Turn the temperature down to 400F and bake for 30 minutes. Then remove the cover and bake for another 40-45 minutes at 380F.

Allow to cool for 15-20 minutes before taking the bread out of the pan. Allow to cool completely before handling or slicing! The longer the better. I usually slice it the next day and freeze it in ziplock bag for up to 4 months. Throw some slices in your toaster whenever you want a sandwich.

Serving size: 1 slice: Calories: 142.4; Total Fat: 4.8 g; Total carbohydrate: 20.3 g; Protein: 4.7 g; Sugars: 0.8 g; Fiber: 5 g; Vitamin A: 0%; Vitamin B-6: 5.3 %; Vitamin C: 0.3 %; Calcium: 2.9 %; Iron: 8.4 %; Magnesium: 6.5 %; Zinc: 3.2 %.

Light Sandwich Bread

Gluten free sourdough sandwich bread with a lighter more delicate texture when compared to other whole grain breads. Still made with healthy wholesome ingredients and without commercial yeast. Also vegan (egg free, dairy free), xanthan gum free and baking powder free.

Makes 1 loaf (15-17 slices)   Ready in 6 hours   GF, DF, V

INGREDIENTS

1 ½ cup sourdough starter, active (see page 280)
3 ½ cups lightweight flour blend (see page 272)
1/2 cup ground flax seeds (golden, for a lighter bread color)
1/4 cup maple sugar
1 ½ tbsp psyllium husk
2 cups filtered water
2 tsp Celtic sea salt
Optional: 1/4 cup oil (or vegan butter for a softer bread)

DIRECTIONS

1. Form the dough. Proceed to this step when the starter is active (bubbling regularly within a few hours of feeding). To the starter add the flours (sifted), psyllium husk, the milled flax seeds, maple sugar and salt. Then add the wet ingredients. Add the water gradually, mix to combine and adjust accordingly. The dough should look like a very thick brownie batter or a thick oatmeal porridge (picture 1). But be careful if it's too thick it will not rise much. If it's too thin it will not bake evenly in the middle, the texture will be more gummy.

Prepare the pan (I used a 9x5" glass pan) by lining it with parchment paper (or at least the bottom), to prevent sticking. Scrape the dough into the pan and smooth it out with a spatula for a nice dome shape (picture 2). Sprinkle seeds or nuts if you want. Cover with a plastic wrap or a towel to seal moisture (spray the inside of the wrap with water to prevent dough from cracking) and let it rise in a warm place approximately 4-5 hours. It depends on how warm is your kitchen.

2. Bake the bread. Preheat oven at 425 degrees F. When ready to bake, remove the wrap, place another heavy bread pan on top that fits tightly (I usually heat it for 10 minutes in the oven first. Giving bread the highest heat possible at the beginning will ensure that the trapped gasses can force the bread to rise quickly). Turn the temperature down to 400F and bake for 30 minutes. Then remove the cover and bake for another 40-45 minutes at 380F.

Allow to cool for 15-20 minutes before taking the bread out of the pan. Cool completely before handling or slicing! The longer the better. I usually slice it the next day and freeze it for up to 4 months. Throw some slices in your toaster whenever you want a sandwich.

Serving size: 1 slice: Calories: 187.2; Total Fat: 2.1 g; Total carbohydrate: 38.9 g; Protein: 3.8 g; Sugars: 2.8 g; Dietary Fiber: 4.1 g; Vitamin B-6: 9.1 %; Calcium: 1.5 %; Iron: 6.3 %; Magnesium: 8.1 %; Zinc: 5.3 %.

Sourdough Hamburger Buns

Simple no-knead vegan gluten free hamburger buns that don't require commercial yeast or shaping skills. The natural fermentation and baking in individual ramekins provides the right crusty exterior and soft interior without being tough or crumbling apart. Easy to slice and toast.

Makes 11 buns   Ready in 6 hours   GF, DF, V

INGREDIENTS

1 ½ cup sourdough starter, active (see page 280)
1 cup oat flour
1 cup buckwheat flour (light)
1/2 cup cassava flour
1/3 cup ground golden flax seeds
1 tbsp psyllium husk
1 ½ cup filtered water
1 ½ tsp Celtic sea salt
1/4 cup maple sugar (optional, or replace with other sweetener)

See recipe video on the blog.

DIRECTIONS

1. Form the dough. Proceed to this step when the starter is active (bubbling regularly within a few hours of feeding).

In a small bowl, whisk together the water, salt and psyllium husk. Let it sit for 2-3 minutes to absorb the water, then pour the content over the starter in another larger bowl.

Then add the rest of the ingredients and mix together until combined, about 2 minutes. Scoop about 1/3 cup of the dough and place into baking cups (4 inch ceramic ramekins) or mini cake ring molds and smooth them out with a spatula (picture 1).

Cover with plastic wrap to seal moisture and allow to ferment at room temperature for 4 to 6 hours, depending how warm is your house. Before baking, brush them with a mixture of olive oil, water and maple syrup (1:1:1), this will form a soft crust and provide a sticky base for the seeds. Sprinkle generously the desired seeds (I used sesame and caraway; picture 2).

2. Bake the buns. Preheat the oven to 380 F. Bake covered (with foil or another baking tray) for 20 minutes, and another 20-25 minutes - uncovered, until browned. Let cool on a wire rack completely, use a knife to detach if necessary (picture 3). Slice in two and freeze for up to 4 months.

Toast to defrost.

Notes And Suggestions

The dough before baking should look like a thick brownie batter or a thick oatmeal porridge. But be careful if it's too thick it will not rise much. If it's too thin it will not bake evenly in the middle, the texture will be more gummy.

Serving size: 1 bun: Calories: 205.7; Total Fat: 3.9 g; Total carbohydrate: 37.1 g; Protein:5.2 g; Sugars: 2.1 g; Dietary Fiber:5.6 g; Vitamin A,C: 0%; Vitamin B-6: 7.7 %; Iron: 7.3 %; Calcium: 7.2 %; Magnesium: 20.1 %; Zinc: 4.3%

257

Sourdough Whole Grain Bread Rolls

No-knead vegan gluten free bread rolls without commercial yeast, gums or other processed ingredients. The natural fermentation provides enough rise and a nice crusty exterior without being too tough to slice. Perfect for burgers, sandwiches or served with soups.

Makes 12 rolls   Ready in 6 hours   GF, DF, V

INGREDIENTS

1 cup sourdough starter, active (see page 280)
2 ¼ flour blend no. 2 (see page 276)
1 tbsp psyllium husk
2 tbsp maple syrup
1 ½ tsp Celtic sea salt
1 cup plant milk (like coconut)
1/4 cup sesame seeds

DIRECTIONS

1. Form the dough. Proceed to this step when the starter is active (bubbling regularly within a few hours of feeding).

In a small bowl, whisk together the plant milk, maple syrup, salt and psyllium husk. Let it sit for 2-3 minutes to thicken then pour the content over the starter in another larger bowl.

Then add the flours (sifted) and mix together until well combined (Image 1).

2. Form the rolls. Prepare a small a mount of oil of your choice to dip in the fingers for a smoother rolling and avoid sticking. Scoop about 1/3 cup of the dough and roll it briefly with your oily hands to form a ball with a nice smooth surface. Place on a large cookie sheet covered with parchment paper. Repeat with remaining dough. Then take some of the sesame seeds with your fingers and gently press them to stick to the rolls surface (Image 2). Cover with plastic wrap or another deep baking dish (Image 3) to seal moisture.

Allow to ferment and rise at room temperature (Image 4) for 4 to 5 hours depending how warm is your house. You can also make the rolls really thin if you prefer your sandwiches / burgers skinny (Image 5), adjust temperature and time.

3. Bake. Preheat the oven to 380 F. Bake for 20 minutes, covered with deep baking pans (in order to allow expansion), then remove and bake uncovered for another 20-25 minutes until browned.

For a crustier crust make sure you use hot preheated pans for covering. Let cool completely on a wire rack, then you can slice in two and freeze for up to 4 months. Throw them in your toaster whenever you want one.

Serving size: 1 roll: Calories: 159.8; Total Fat: 3.2 g; Total carbohydrate: 27.6 g; Protein: 3.7 g; Sugars: 3.5 g; Dietary Fiber: 3 g; Vitamin B-6: 7 %; Vitamin A & C: 0 %; Iron: 6 %; Calcium: 7.3 %; Magnesium: 16.6%; Zinc: 4.8 %.

| Breads Rolls Tortillas

Grain Free Banana Bread

Moist, fluffy with cinnamon flavor, naturally sweetened banana bread by the ripe bananas and dates plus studded with crunchy walnuts. This nutritious banana bread is one of the most delicious comfort foods you can have! Enjoy it as dessert, snack or breakfast.

Yields 10 slices   Ready in 1h 10 minutes   GF, DF, P, W30

INGREDIENTS

4 medium eggs
4 medium bananas, mashed
1/4 cup vegan butter
2 cups grain free flour mix (see page 278)
2 tbsp coconut flour
3/4 cup walnuts, finely chopped
6 Medjool dates, soaked, pitted and chopped
1 tsp baking soda + 1 tsp apple cider vinegar
1/3 tsp sea salt
2/3 tsp cinnamon powder

Optional:

3 tbsp finely chopped walnuts + 3 tbsp maple sugar (to sprinkle over the bread)

DIRECTIONS

1. Preheat the oven to 360 F. Use parchment paper to line a 9x5 inch loaf pan.

2. Mash the bananas with a fork in a mixing bowl. Add the eggs, vegan butter or coconut oil, and mix until fully combined. Then add the chopped dates (or other dried fruit) walnuts, and give it a gentle mix.

3. To that add the flour (sifted), cinnamon, salt and mix just enough to combine. Do not over-mix. At the end add the baking soda and the apple cider vinegar to produce leavening. Gently mix and pour in the pan.

4. Cook the bread for 60 minutes total. To avoid cracking and produce a nice rise, cover the bread with another loaf pan for the first 20 minutes, then remove it.

Notes And Suggestions

Cool completely before slicing. The bread will be too soft and gooey when it's warm. Its texture will firm up as it cools.

The bread will last for a few days covered at room temperature, or up to a week in the refrigerator. And will keep well frozen for up to 3 months.

Serving size: 1 slice: Calories: 303.1; Total Fat: 13.7 g; Total carbohydrate: 43.2 g; Protein: 5.7 g; Sugars: 18.8 g; Dietary Fiber: 6.6g; Calcium: 3.4 %; Iron: 5.2 %; Vitamin A: 3.7 %; Vitamin B-6: 19.5 %; Vitamin C: 7.5 %; Magnesium: 9.3 %; Zinc: 5 %.

Sourdough Cranberry Banana Bread

A healthy sourdough eggless banana bread that is soft, moist and doesn't fall apart when cut. It's also dairy free, oil free and refined sugar free. This recipe is perfect for using the sourdough discard when feeding your gluten free sourdough starter.

Makes 1 loaf (12 slices)   Ready in 1 h 30 minutes   GF, DF, V

INGREDIENTS

1 cup gluten free sourdough starter, active
1/2 cup oat flour
1/2 cup tigernut flour, or almond flour
1/4 cup cassava flour
1/3 cup ground flax seeds
1 cup non-dairy milk
3 medium bananas, mashed
1 cup dried cranberries
1/2 tsp pink salt
1 tsp cinnamon
1 tsp vanilla extract
3/4 tsp baking soda
3/4 tsp apple cider vinegar

Optional for sprinkling

2 tbsp sesame seeds
2 tbsp coconut shreds
1 tsp maple sugar

DIRECTIONS

Preheat oven to 400 F. Cover a 10x4 inch loaf pan with parchment paper. Set aside.

1. Form the dough. In a bowl, combine the bananas with plant milk, vanilla extract and cranberries. Set aside. Meanwhile in another large bowl, combine the starter, the flours (sifted), baking soda, cinnamon, ground flax seeds and salt. Gently mix the banana mixture with dry ingredients. At the end add the apple cider vinegar and give it a final gentle mix. Pour the batter into the prepared loaf pan. If desired, sprinkle the top with maple sugar, seeds and coconut shreds or other preferred toppings. Cover with a towel, or platic wrap and let it rise for about 15-20 min in a warm place (not too hot). If you're not using baking soda, let it ferment for aprox. 4 hours or until it rises a bit.

2. Bake the banana bread. When baking, cover with a piece of aluminum foil (or other bread pan) for the first 30 minutes. Then lower the temperature from 400 F to 370 F and remove the covering. Bake for another 35-40 minutes, until a toothpick inserted into the center comes out clean. Allow to cool before removing from the pan. Set on a rack to cool completely and slice. I keep it frozen (pre-sliced) and whenever I need I just throw a few slices in the toaster. The smell is extraordinary and it tastes like it was just baked.

Notes And Suggestions

If you can't have oat flour, use buckwheat flour instead.

The recipe and video with instructions also available on the blog.

Serving size: 1 slice: Calories: 169.5; Total Fat:6 g; Total carbohydrate: 32.5 g; Protein:4.1 g; Sugars:12.3 g; Dietary Fiber: 3.2 g; Vitamin A: 2.3 %; Vitamin B-6: 13.8 %; Vitamin C: 9.9 %; Iron: 6.2 %; Calcium: 9.1 %; Magnesium: 17.6 %.

Gluten Free Sourdough Pizza

For this no yeast (no baking powder) pizza dough, you need a gluten free sourdough starter but it requires minimal effort and you just wait the fermentation process to do it's job. At the end you get a a delicious gluten free crusty pizza and without a soggy bottom.

Makes 1 (10") pizza   Ready in 3h 30 minutes   GF, DF, V

INGREDIENTS

Pizza crust:

1 cup gluten free sourdough starter, active (see page 280)

1/2 cup white rice flour

1/4 cup arrowroot powder

1 tbsp non-dairy milk

1 tsp psyllium husk

2 tsp maple sugar

1/4 cup melted vegan butter (I used Miyoko's)

1/2 tsp sea salt

Toppings:

4 tbsp BBQ sauce (see page 238)

1/2 bell pepper, sliced

1/4 cup eggplant dip (see page 74)

1/4 small red onion, sliced

3 baby bella mushrooms, sliced

1 scallion, chopped

Note:

For people who can't imagine a pizza without cheese - Violife dairy free cheese is a good alternative, otherwise is best to avoid highly processed products.

DIRECTIONS

1. In a cup mix together the psyllium husk, the melted butter and milk, then add mixture to the sourdough starter (active with bubbles), gently mix until incorporated then add the other ingredients and form a soft dough (like a soft play dough).

2. Place the dough on a piece of parchment paper and press with your fingers to form a flattened thin disk (about 10-12" in diameter), or use a rolling pin. Cover with cling wrap to seal moisture and let it rise in dark warm place for 3 to 4 hours.

3. Towards the end of the rise time, preheat the oven to 400 F. When ready to bake, slide the parchment paper and dough (without cling wrap) on a preheated cookie sheet right into the oven. Bake for 15 minutes.

4. Then remove from oven, sauce and top as you like and place it back for another 15 minutes. Bake until the crust is brown and the toppings are cooked through.

5. As toppings, in the photo I used BBQ sauce (or use some basil pesto (page 234) or cauliflower cream (page 240), bell peppers, red onion, mushrooms, scallions and few teaspoons of my eggplant dip (see page 74).

Notes And Suggestions

To prevent cracking and get a high rise we need to cover the pizza dough for the first 10 minutes in the oven - this prevents moisture loss. And for a crispier top I like to turn on the broiler for the last 1 minute of baking.

If you don't mind a slightly darker color of the dough, try and other flour blends from the book.

Serving size: 1 slice (crust only): Calories: 152.3; Total Fat: 5.8 g; Total carbohydrate: 27.6 g; Protein: 2.1 g; Sugars: 0.8 g; Dietary Fiber: 1.6 g; Vitamin A: 0 %; Vitamin B-6: 9.4 %; Vitamin C: 0 %; Iron: 2.5 %; Calcium: 0.7 %.

Gluten Free Sourdough Naan Flatbread

This is an easy skillet cooked Indian style flat-bread that is soft and pliable, almost like the real one but without commercial yeast or xanthan gum. No need to wait, knead or roll out. Perfect for snacking with dips, pair with soups, or use as a base for mini pizzas and wraps.

Makes 10 naans   Ready in 45 minutes   GF, DF, V

INGREDIENTS

1 ½ cup gluten free sourdough starter, active (see page 280)
1/2 cup oat flour, gluten free
1/2 cup arrowroot powder
1/2 cup cassava flour
2 tsp psyllium husk
3 tbsp ground golden flax seeds
2 ½ cup non-dairy milk
1/4 cup melted vegan butter
1 tsp Celtic sea salt
1 tsp baking soda
1 tsp apple cider vinegar
1 tsp avocado oil (for frying each naan)

Optional sprinkle:

onion powder
dried parsley
dried basil
dried rosemary

DIRECTIONS

1. In a large mixing bowl, add the gluten free sourdough starter (I used some starter that was supposed to be discarded - when feeding a new batch), non-dairy milk, psyllium husk, ground flax seeds and salt. Mix to combine and let it sit for 10 minutes so the seeds could soak up the milk.

2. Then add the oat flour, cassava flour and arrowroot powder. Give it a thorough mix. At the end mix in the melted vegan butter.

3. Preheat a skillet on medium-high heat, brush with oil before cooking each naan.

4. While the skillet is heating add the final 2 ingredients in the batter: baking soda and apple cider vinegar (or lemon juice). This will create the leavening action needed for puffiness. But don't over-mix, just enough to combine. This will look more like a thick pancake batter than a dough (picture 1).

5. Drop about 1/2 cup of the batter on the skillet. Spread into an oval (7") using a spatula or by rotating and wiggling until you get the desired thickness (picture 2). I like them thinner. Cook for about 2-3 minutes until golden. Sprinkle with desired herbs and seasoning just before flipping on the other side.

6. Remove on a baking sheet covered with parchment paper. Repeat with each naan until you're done.

7. For making sure the middle is cooked properly place the baking sheet with naans (arranged in a single layer (picture 3) - covered with foil) in a preheated oven at 380F for 10-15 minutes (to prevent moisture loss), and uncovered for another 5 minutes.

If you prefer them crispier, bake them uncovered and longer.

Notes And Suggestions

Buckwheat or sorghum flour is a good alternative to oat flour.
Keep batter thinner and spread thinner for more pliable naans.

Serving size: 1 naan: Calories: 213; Total Fat: 7.2 g; Total carbohydrate: 35.7 g; Protein: 3.4 g; Sugars: 0.2 g; Dietary Fiber: 4.1 g; Vitamin A: 0 %; Vitamin B-6: 0 %; Vitamin C: 0 %; Iron: 3.5 %; Calcium: 3.6 %; Magnesium: 7.3 %.

Gluten Free Sourdough Baguette

This "yeast free" baguettes have a crusty golden exterior and a classic, chewy crumb, just like the real ones. Theres is no need to knead, or use a mixer. Create a sub sandwich, enjoy it with a bowl of soup or with your favorite spreads.

Makes 2 baguettes   Ready in 6 hours   GF, DF

INGREDIENTS

1 cup gluten free sourdough starter, active (see page 280)
3/4 cup sweet brown rice flour
3/4 cup + 2 tbsp sorghum flour
1/2 cup arrowroot powder
1 ½ tbsp psyllium husk
4 tbsp ground golden flax seeds
1 ⅓ cup non-dairy milk
2 large egg whites
2 tbsp honey (optional)
1 ½ tsp Celtic sea salt

DIRECTIONS

1. In a large mixing bowl, add the gluten free sourdough starter (active, room temperature), non-dairy milk, egg whites (slightly beaten), honey, psyllium husk, ground flax seeds and salt. Mix.

2. Add the flours. Give it another mix using a spatula. The dough will look more like a thick, stiff batter than a dough (picture 1).

3. To shape the baguette take a plastic food wrap, spoon on it half the dough. Fold in one side of the wrap and roll, smooth it out with your hands into an elongated shape: 14" long, 2" wide (picture 2).

4. Cover a French baguette pan with parchment paper, and transfer the shaped baguette on it: sliding (unrolling) from the plastic wrap right onto it. Proceed the same with the second one.

5. Cover them with a lightly greased plastic wrap (picture 3) and place in warm dark space, like your turned off oven, that was previously used. It shouldn't be hot, just somewhere between 80-85 degrees F. A higher temperature could kill the yeast. Let them rise for 4 to 5 hours, until almost doubled in size (picture 4).

6. When ready, take them out, and preheat the oven to 450 F. Right before placing into the oven, slash each baguette with a razor (optional) and spray with cool water in a spray bottle. This will help with creating a nice crust.

7. Place the baking sheet a bit higher than the center of the oven and throw a couple of ice cubes on the bottom of the oven to create more steam. Bake for 20 minutes than rotate the pan, lower the temperature to 375 F and bake for another 15-20 minutes. If you want a softer crust, wrap them in a towel right after you take them out. Let cool completely before slicing.

Notes And Suggestions

Egg whites are essential in this recipe as they keep the texture fluffier and less gummy. Sweet brown rice flour can be replaced by oat flour or buckwheat flour. But the texture and taste will change a bit.

Serving size: 1/2 baguette: Calories: 505.1; Total Fat: 6.5 g; Total carbohydrate: 99.3 g; Protein: 12.2 g; Sugars: 6.2 g; Dietary Fiber: 11.1 g; Vitamin A: 0 %; Vitamin B-6: 25.5 %; Vitamin C: 0 %; Iron: 10 %; Calcium: 3.6 %; Magnesium: 21.7 %; Zinc: 11.4 %.

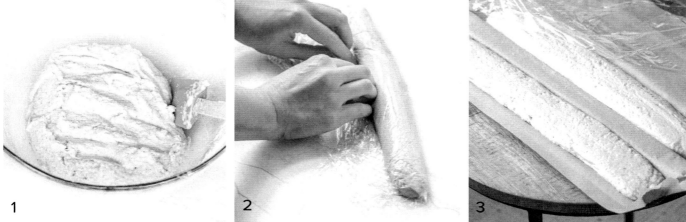

1

2

3

269

Miscellaneous

• •

This section comprises recipes for gluten free flour mixes including wholegrain flour and grain free flour, without highly processed starches and gums. Each mix presented in this book is devised to work for a variety of baked goods, from fluffy light cakes to denser hearty baked goods and darker in color.

Most gluten free flour blends contain up to 40-50% added starch, like cornstarch (usually made from genetically modified corn) or potato starch and with added gums. These unhealthy ingredients actually create more digestive discomfort for some people. Therefore in my recipes I try to use only good quality (organic) whole grain flours, with some healthier added starches, like cassava flour or arrowroot flour. Cassava flour is not tapioca flour, it is made from the entire root and is less processed.

Gluten Free Dairy Free Tips In Baking And Cooking

Substitutes for gums: Gums hold the ingredients together, act like a glue, providing elasticity. The most popular are xanthan gum (often derived from corn) and guar gum (legume derived). A great natural alternative to gums for those with intolerances, is psyllium husk (the whole psyllium husk seeds work better than the powder) and ground flax seeds or a combination of both. These two are plant derived, high in fiber and so their addition in baked goods will require more liquid. If you want a lighter color try using golden flax seeds. And grind them yourself because the flax meals sold in stores have a rather coarse consistency.

Measure it correctly: It is best to spoon the flour mixture into a measuring cup and level off with a knife, and try to avoid tapping the flour. Also make sure to use sifted flour in order to avoid large lumps.

Dairy substitutions: Most people use highly processed nutritionless vegan butters (margarines). They usually contain soybean, palm fruit, canola, and other cheap oils, among added flavors, additives and preservatives. All these are detrimental for our health, whether we have intolerances or not. The cleanest list of ingredients seems to have: Miyoko's (which is what I usually use) - a cultured vegan butter mainly made from coconut oil and cashews. It has a firm, sliceable texture and performs well in baking and cooking. They also recently released a nut free version - oat milk - for those allergic to nuts. Another great simple option is pure coconut oil.

As for dairy free yogurt, there are tons of brands as well, but again they all contain thickeners and additives. The ones I like to use (because they have a cleaner ingredients list without gums) are from Harmless Harvest or CoYo (richer but is harder to find in stores).

There are many varieties of non-dairy milks as well, but I couldn't find one that is "clean" enough to consume, or it has an odd taste and texture. Therefore I'm making my own by combining canned coconut milk with homemade tigernut milk (see page 202). It's rich, slightly sweet and tasty by itself, plus it performs well in all of my recipes. If you really need a good store-bought non dairy milk, those from Forager (coconut cashew based milk) and Malk (almond based milk) have a "cleaner" ingredient list than a majority of them.

Lightweight Gluten Free Flour Blend

A lighter gluten free flour mix (pastry flour) that has the ability to create a fluffier texture to those baked goods that need a more delicate structure. Great for cakes, pie crusts, cupcakes, crepes or delicate cookies. No tapioca, potato starch or xanthan gum here.

Makes 3 ⅓ cups   Ready in 5 minutes   GF, DF, V

INGREDIENTS

1 cup (167g) brown rice flour
1 cup (121g) sorghum flour
2/3 cup (81g) cassava flour
2/3 cup (85g) arrowroot flour

DIRECTIONS

1. Add the flours to a large mixing bowl.
2. Mix until fully combined.

Notes And Suggestions

Store flour mix in an airtight container up to 1-2 weeks.

For longer storage, store in the refrigerator to prevent rancidity. You can store a portion of it in an airtight container at room temperature and refrigerate the rest for later use.

Use as a 1:1 replacement for flour or all-purpose gluten free flour blends.

Gluten free flour does not rise like regular flour so you will need to add leavening agents like baking soda + an acid or baking powder. I don't recommend adding those to your main flour. Instead, add them when the recipe requires.

For extra binding properties you can add 1-2 tbsp of flax meal or psyllium husk, especially when you don't use eggs.

If you want the best quality possible - choose organic flours made from sprouted whole grains and minimally processed.

Serving size: 1 cup and 2 tbsp: Calories: 551.8; Total Fat: 3.1 g; Total carbohydrate: 119.3 g; Protein: 12.1 g; Sugars: 0.4 g; Dietary Fiber: 8.2 g; Vitamin B-6: 19.5 %; Calcium: 1.7 %; Magnesium: 15 %; Iron: 6.4 %; Zinc: 8.7 %.

| Miscellaneous / Flours

Whole Grain Gluten Free Flour Blend 1

A gluten free flour mix high in protein and fiber, made from real whole grains – no added starches. Bake hearty, rustic whole grain breads, rolls, pizza crust, flat breads or crackers but expect a slightly darker color. Great for recipes where other bold flavors will stand up against it.

Makes 3 cups + 3 tbsp   Ready in 5 minutes   GF, DF, V

INGREDIENTS

1 ⅓ cup (160g) buckwheat flour
1 cup (120g) teff flour
2/3 cup (100g) brown rice flour
3 tbsp (20g) flaxseed meal

DIRECTIONS

1. Add the flours to a large mixing bowl.
2. Mix until fully combined.

Notes And Suggestions

Store flour mix in an airtight container up to 1-2 weeks.

For longer storage, store in the refrigerator to prevent rancidity. You can store a portion of it in an airtight container at room temperature and refrigerate the rest for later use.

You can also make your own (lighter in color) buckwheat flour from raw buckwheat groats, by using a high speed blender.

Gluten free flour does not rise like regular flour so you will need to add leavening agents like baking soda + an acid or baking powder. I don't recommend adding those to your main flour. Instead, add them when the recipe requires.

For extra binding properties you can add 1 tbsp of psyllium husk.

If you want the best quality possible - choose organic flours made from sprouted whole grains and minimally processed.

Serving size: 1 cup and 1 tbsp: Calories: 461.3; Total Fat: 6.6 g; Total carbohydrate: 84.5 g; Protein: 16.1 g; Sugars: 1.6 g; Dietary Fiber: 17 g; Iron: 13.9 %; Calcium: 1.4 %; Magnesium: 9.7 %.

Whole Grain Gluten Free Flour Blend 2

A gluten free flour blend of real whole grain flours – no added starches. Yields lighter-colored baked goods than the wholegrain blend no. 1. Great for all kind of breads, denser cakes, crackers, muffins and cookies.

Makes 2 ¼ cups   Ready in 5 minutes   GF, DF, V

INGREDIENTS

3/4 cup (75 g) oat flour (gluten free)
1/2 cup (61g) sorghum flour
1/2 cup (79g) white rice flour
3 tbsp (20g) flaxseed meal

DIRECTIONS

1. Add the flours to a large mixing bowl.
2. Mix until fully combined.

Notes And Suggestions

1. Store flour mix in an airtight container up to 1-2 weeks.

2. For longer storage, store in the refrigerator to prevent rancidity. You can store a portion of it in an airtight container at room temperature and refrigerate the rest for later use.

3. Use as a replacement for the lightweight flour blend if you want only whole grains and less starches in your baked goods.

4. Gluten free flour does not rise like regular flour so you will need to add leavening agents like baking soda + an acid or baking powder. Add them when the recipe requires.

5. You can replace the oat flour with millet flour (make sure is not rancid, or it will have a bitter taste), in case you are intolerant to oats. Make your own oat flour by milling gluten free rolled oats in a high speed blender.

6. For extra binding properties you can add 1 tbsp of psyllium husk. If you want a lighter color, use golden flaxseed meal instead of brown.

Serving size: 1 cup: Calories: 460.9; Total Fat: 8.4 g; Total carbohydrate: 84.3 g; Protein: 14.1 g; Sugars: 0.3 g; Dietary Fiber: 9.4 g; Iron: 13.2 %; Calcium: 22.5%; Magnesium: 57.4 %.

| Miscellaneous / Flours

Gluten & Grain Free Flour Blend

A gluten free flour blend without grains. Great as a cup-for-cup replacement for all-purpose flour. Use for cakes, cookies, muffins, paleo pancakes, flatbreads, crackers, scones, pizza crust and more. Nut free version included!

Makes aprox. 2 cups   Ready in 5 minutes   GF, DF, V, P, W30

INGREDIENTS

1 cup + 2 tbsp (145g) cassava flour
1/4 cup (32g) arrowroot powder
2/3 cup (64g) almond flour

For nut free version replace the almond flour with 1/2 cup (60g) tigernut flour

DIRECTIONS

1. Add the flours to a large mixing bowl.
2. Mix until fully combined.

Notes And Suggestions

Store flour mix in an airtight container up to 1-2 weeks.

For longer storage, store in the refrigerator to prevent rancidity. You can store a portion of it in an airtight container at room temperature and refrigerate the rest for later use.

Use as a 1:1 replacement for other gluten free flour blends.

Gluten free flour does not rise like regular flour so you will need to add leavening agents like baking soda + an acid or baking powder. Add them when the recipe requires.

You can replace the arrowroot flour with green banana flour (it performs like a starch and doesn't have a banana taste) in case you are intolerant.

Tigernut flour is one of my favorite flours (I always choose it over almond flour), it's nutritious, nut free, full of fiber, slightly sweet in taste and it produces airy baked goods when properly combined with other flours.

Serving size: 1 cup: Calories: 490.5; Total Fat: 18.4 g; Total carbohydrate: 74.6 g; Protein: 10 g; Sugars: 1.3 g; Dietary Fiber: 8.6 g; Iron: 8.2 %; Calcium: 8.5%; Vitamin E: 46.2 %; Magnesium: 26.5 %.

| Miscellaneous / Flours

Gluten Free Sourdough Starter

If I want to avoid eggs, gums, thickeners, baking powder, and dairy products, this gluten free sourdough starter is the base for almost all my gluten free baked goods. Nothing else can be substituted with the same results if you want a natural leavening effect. The starter is a living version of commercial yeast (but healthier), maintained with a mix of flour and water.

INGREDIENTS

DIRECTIONS Ready in 7-9 days GF, DF, V

You will need:

1 packet of dehydrated Sourdough starter culture (from brown rice, find it on Amazon)
filtered water
brown rice flour (you will need about 40 oz total)

(I'm using organic sprouted brown rice flour; regular brown rice flour works too.)

Equipment:

2 qt glass jar
mixing spatula
muslin or cotton cloth
rubber band (to secure)

Please see a video tutorial and more troubleshooting on the blog.

1. In the jar add 1 tbsp flour and 1 tbsp of filtered water (room temperature) then add the packet of starter and stir thoroughly. If it feels too thick to mix, add 1 tsp more water. It should look like a paste. Cover the jar with a cloth and secure with rubber band. Leave in a warm place (75-80°F is ideal) for 24 hours.

2. After 24 hours, feed the starter with 2 tbsp of flour and 2 tbsp of water. Stir thoroughly. Cover and let it ferment for another 18-24 hours.

3. Feed the starter again: 1/4 cup of flour + 1/4 cup water. Stir and cover.

4. After 12-14 hours, you might start to see some bubbles. Feed it again with an additional ½ cup of flour and ½ cup water. Stir thoroughly.

5. After 12-14 hours discard all but ½ cup starter and then feed the starter again with ½ cup water and ½ cup flour. Stir thoroughly.

6. Repeat step 5 every 8 hours for 3-5 days or until the starter is bubbling regularly within 4 hours of feeding. It means your starter is activated and ready to use. At this point, use the amount of starter you need and place the rest in the refrigerator until ready to use. From here you can feed it just once a week, without discarding anything.

Remember: the golden feeding ratio is: 1 part starter to 1 part flour and 1 part water (by volume).

Notes And Suggestions

1. If you want to avoid discarding in the trash, then separate into another container and use it later (the same week) in a recipe: cakes, muffins, pancakes, use it in place of yogurt or sour cream or even milk.

2. Every time you want to use your starter for baking, pull it out and feed it the night before (or at least 4 hours in advance) to awaken it's activity. Once you've added the starter to your recipe, feed the remaining starter and return to the refrigerator.

3. The wild yeast in your starter thrives in warm temperatures, and it will take longer to culture in cool climates. If within the first 4 days of starting the starter it doesn't develop a lot of bubbles and starts to form a layer of liquid on top - is a sign that is needing more food and getting too hungry faster. **The problem:** it's not being fed enough and/or often enough. **Solve it:** pour the liquid off, then discard most of the starter (like in step 6) and adjust your feeding schedule accordingly. If a second feeding doesn't work, you can increase to a 1:2:2 feeding ratio.

Weights & Measures

Note that the calculations of spoons / cups to grams will vary according to the density of the ingredient and how it is packed into the cup

	US VOLUME	METRIC VOLUME	METRIC WEIGHT
1 TEASPOON (TSP) OR 1/3 TBSP	1/6 FL OZ	5 ml	4.5 grams
1 TABLESPOON (TBSP)	1/2 FL OZ	15 ml	14 grams
2 TABLESPOONS	1 FL OZ	30 ml	29 grams
4 TBSP (1/4 CUP)	2 FL OZ	60 ml	57 grams
1/3 CUP	2.7 FL OZ	80 ml	76 grams
1/2 CUP	4.05 FL OZ	119 ml	114 grams
3/4 CUP	6.08 FL OZ	180 ml	171 grams
1 CUP	8.1 FL OZ	240 ml	229 grams
1 PINT (2 CUPS)	16 FL OZ	473.18 ml	458 grams
1 QUART (4 CUPS)	32 FL OZ	946.36 ml	920 grams

The charts use standard U.S. measures and offer equivalents for United States and metric measures. All measurements are approximate and most have been rounded up or down to the nearest whole number.

Make sure that you have actual commercial measuring utensils: measuring cups to use for measuring dry ingredients and measuring spoons; your stainless coffee spoon is not going to give accurate measurements.

For liquid ingredients, you need a clear glass or plastic cup with a pouring spout and measuring marks.

Oven Temperatures

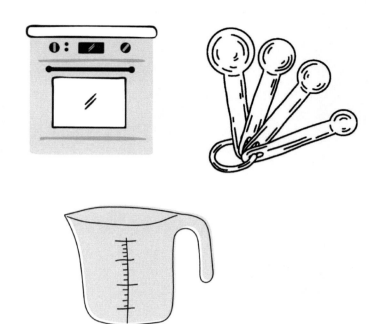

US	METRIC
250° F	121° C
300° F	149° C
350° F	177° C
400° F	204° C
450° F	232° C
500° F	260 ° C

Measures for Pans & Dishes

	INCHES	CENTIMETERS
BAKING DISH	9x13	22x33
BAKING DISH	8x8	20x20
LOAF PAN	9x5	23x12
BAKING DISH	9x9	22x22
CAKE PAN ROUND	10	25
CAKE PAN ROUND	6	15
COOKIE SHEET	16.5x11	42x28